when money is **NOT** above everything

This work was supported by FCT, I.P., the Portuguese national funding agency for science, research and technology, under the Project UIDB/04521/2020.

when
money
is
NOT
above
everything

other ways of working, generating income, and living

Igor Valentim

ComPassos Coletivos
2020

ComPassos Coletivos
livros@compassoscoletivos.com.br
Rio de Janeiro | Brasil
Worldwide distribution

All the photos are the authors'.

Publisher's Cataloging-in-Publication data

Valentim, Igor Vinicius Lima, 1980 –
When money is not above everything: other ways of working, generating income, and living/ Igor Vinicius Lima Valentim.

Includes references and index.
Includes images.

ISBN (EPUB edition): 978-65-00-04424-9
ISBN (Kindle edition): 978-65-991339-0-9
ISBN (paperback edition): 978-65-991339-1-6

1. Social Sciences. 2. Qualitative Research. 3. Cartography 4. Cooperativism. 5. Capitalism. I. Title.
V155w   CDU 334.012.34

For Elza and Genaro,
my eternal references

CONTENTS

FOREWORD

Can we still dream of a more egalitarian and fairer world? Do we want it?

Can we find now, in our current time, concrete examples of people living and working in different settings than corporations and profit-oriented organizations? Do we want to?

Is there something different going on? Or is it all just a utopia portrayed in books and movies?

We live the imperative of winning: always and at any price. Results matter, but not how we get to them. We do not see ourselves as complementary or interdependent. The other human beings have become adversaries, competitors... enemies! Everyone must survive, behave, and thrive according to this logic.

What shocks me most is how many of us consider this kind of mindset, policies, and ways of life to be natural. People aspire to grow more and more within these ready and available ideals of success. Success for whom? At the cost of whom?

Me first. Me second. Me third. But that is not unanimous!
Not everyone thinks, feels, and desires to live like this!

I always get confused when I think that we are in the middle of the 21st century, with so much technology, so many resources of all kinds, so many possibilities of making the world a better place for everybody and not just for a tiny group, and we still consider that the 'standard' way to work, generate income, find the necessary means to live, is to fit within the model that is the most common: to work in highly hierarchical, utilitarian private companies, where one commands and the others obey, where people are managed by fear of losing their job (and livelihood) the next day.

By the way, how is it possible that, in the same organization, one earns a thousand times more than the other? How can this be supported, applauded, justified, and even desired by so many people? There is no search for egalitarianism, but, on the contrary, a stimulus to the competition.

Or you can struggle to become an entrepreneur, a successful entrepreneur, which is again an option focused on individualism and on winning alone - or almost alone - in this wild world of money and success.

Something that I often think about is: what do we stimulate when we adhere to determined values, practices, and behaviors? What are we signalizing as natural, as positive? What are we (re)producing?

Does anyone want to work based on collaboration, to design and implement policies to distribute wealth more equally inside their organizations and societies?

There are other - not so publicized - ways of living, working, generating income, establishing relationships. Of seeing the world and ourselves.

How, then, is it possible to live, work and generate income in more collective and less hierarchical ways than in traditional companies? How to work in organizations in which income is more equally distributed among all and all? Where decisions are more participatory, and things decided more collectively?

Is there someone building ways of working and generating income collectively supported by values such as solidarity, participation, and equality?

I am sure there are other ways of living and working.
How and where can I find them?

I was not always an academic. I started working at the age of 17 and I have had jobs in the financial department of a computer company, investment banking, financial consulting company, language school, and even in the food industry. I have only started a new life and career as an academic when I had just turned 29.

In all these work experiences, I was bothered by things such as treating hierarchy as a supreme and unquestionable value, both openly in a military-based organizational culture where one determines monocratically and the others just obey, and also in several 'modern' private companies where **supposedly** the hierarchy is left behind if relations are apparently horizontal.

Yes, supposedly. Why do I say that? Because at the end of the day, as much as relationships are more dialogued, participatory, people are more heard (which is all super positive), let us not be mistaken: we live in a capitalist world. And in this world, whoever has the power to fire you and put you out on the street without just cause and, consequently, leave you without money to eat, there is no negotiation possible. Either you do what they expect of you, what others need and desire, what others think is necessary, or you are out. This is called employability: being useful for some organizations. In the light and mild way, with beautiful words, or the hard way, with the words whipping us.

What have always shocked me most is how many of us consider these modes of working, living, and being, aiming to grow more and more within this scenario, something natural.

It is rare to perceive incentives to collective mobilization, ways of managing life, and organizations that stimulate values such as cooperation, solidarity, and egalitarianism.

We cannot fail to question and even deconstruct what seems to represent the nature of people and things, including to show that the modes of existence are neither unique nor inevitable.

I did not want to just complain. Denouncing, debating, discussing: all fundamental. But I wanted to go further. I was curious to look for concrete alternatives. Practical possibilities. Concrete experiences. To live. To experiment.

Until 2004, I had never heard of Solidarity Economy, associativism, or even self-management. But there are initiatives in which profit does not seem to be above all. You must pick them up, listen to them. You must live them.

I sometimes think I have had a kind of nomadic life. Since I left Rio de Janeiro for the first time, I have lived in different Brazilian cities such as Porto Alegre, Balneário Camboriú, Itajaí, Criciúma, Itapiranga, Ribeirão Preto. I have also lived in Lisbon, Portugal, and on an island in the middle of the Atlantic Ocean: São Miguel island, in the Azores.

I love listening to stories and dreams. I love learning from how people build their existences and what types of values and societies these modes stimulate. It was essential to meet people who, together, fight for other ways of working and being, based on attitudes and values that are more loving and focused on life than those who today seem naturalized to many people, but that have nothing of natural.

I walked through streets and avenues, talked to university professors, civil servants of various levels and institutions, and workers from different NGOs and companies, as well as with lots of 'anonymous'.

I write this book with narratives linked to what I lived and felt: processes, experiences, experimentations. Theory is treated here as a tool, not as an end. This book can also be a tool. I share collectively built paths, by myself and all those with whom I have met over the past few years. I try hard to make it a job with and not about people and companies.

I have learned a lot. I took many life lessons. During my journeys, I have heard and witnessed something that seems contrary to what many preach and believe:

"there are other suppliers... other qualities of dough. Everybody must win. Everyone must sell. Everyone must have their space."

I hope that this book can affect you, raise questions, concerns, actions, and changes, especially in the direction of more just, egalitarian, and supportive worlds.

PREFACE

José Maria Carvalho Ferreira[1]

Epistemological and methodological controversies about Solidarity Economy have been the subject of quarrels and conflicts, most of the time, spurious. The institutionalization and legitimation of the Solidary Economy concept cross three major types of difficulties. First, the identity and specificity of the concept are confronted, several times, with others such as Third Sector and Social Economy. Secondly, it is important to understand the degree of development achieved by the curricular structures of the courses that integrate Solidarity Economy in secondary and tertiary education. Thirdly, it is essential to know the social plasticity of the concrete experiences that remain worldwide and claim the status of Solidarity Economy.

The relevance and timeliness of the theme of Solidarity Economy are very well elaborated by Igor Valentim. Thus, early on, the author formulates questions about the alienating character of undergraduate and graduate education in management schools of public and private universities, highlighting the instrumentalization and objectives of this teaching in the sense of profit and exploitation of people by people. On the other hand, there is still an alienation regarding the experimentation of practical experiences that emerge outside the walls of universities. For Igor Valentim, there are significant examples of these experiences in Brazil and Portugal.

Solidarity Economy, in its epistemological and methodological distinctiveness, according to the author, can be visualized from three basic assumptions: self-management, egalitarianism, and solidarity.

Although the historical character of the concepts of egalitarianism and

---

1 Professor, SOCIUS/ISEG, University of Lisbon, Portugal.

solidarity are rooted in the French revolution, their social experimentation emerges fundamentally from the mid-nineteenth century in Western Europe and later in the USA and other more developed capitalist countries. In most cases, these social experiences were thought and lived in terms of the radical transformation of global societies.

The examples of the Commune of Paris of 1971, the Russian revolution of 1905 and 1917, the revolution in Spain of 1936-39, May 1968, and others, equate and configure very well the content of the economic, social, political and cultural changes that emerged in these contexts. Of course, the manifestations of egalitarianism and solidarity were also present in the microsocial realities. Cooperatives, mutual aid associations, savings banks, and mutual societies have in many cases been unequivocal demonstrations of this solidarity and egalitarianism.

Concerning self-management, its observance and historical representativeness fall within the twentieth century, especially in the experiences carried out by the Soviets in the Russian revolution of 1905 and 1917 and the Spanish revolution of 1936-39. Self-management, in the broad sense of the term, proved to be a modality of individual and collective autonomous action, and free lived by workers and peasants, without any hierarchical power above this freedom and autonomy. The decision-making process and the leadership process and, logically, the execution of tasks and functions were referred to as a sphere of action based on turnover, spontaneity, and informality.

Today, when we write or talk about self-management, egalitarianism, and solidarity, we are constrained to clarify the specificity and heuristic value of the concept of Solidarity Economy. In this aspect, Igor Valentim problematizes the concept of self-management by making the counterpoint with the concept of heteromanagement. For the author of this book, heteromanagement means a type of experience and practice of economic activity based on the laws of regulation of the market and the State, striving for competition and competition and the struggle for profit. It is a type of normative management of capitalist companies, and it is at the top of the organizational pyramid of hierarchical authority that decisions and leadership are developed. We are in the presence of a model of social relations guided by the law of the strongest in the hierarchical exercise of power over information, energy, and knowledge that forms the functioning of any capitalist company.

From Igor Valentim's perspective, self-management is the denial of heteromanagement, to the extent that the socialization of power within interpersonal, intragroup, intergroup, and intraorganizational relationships is crossed by direct democracy. The horizontality of social relations obeys a spontaneous and informal logic. Thus, the process of producing goods develops in the sense of the production of affective, egalitarian, and solidary sociability. Direct democracy happens by becoming the structuring factor of self-management. On the other hand, it leads to the emergence of egalitarianism and solidarity.

In the readings and case studies experienced by Igor Valentim, it was possible to build an analysis model called Solidarity Economy. However, in my opinion, there is a problem which is essential to clarify. It is important to understand the extent to which there are antinomies or similarities between the concepts of representative democracy, participatory democracy, and direct democracy.

If we write or speak of the concepts of self-management, egalitarianism, and solidarity in the profound sense of terms, if we consider Solidarity Economy to be based on representative democracy or participatory democracy, the assumptions of the social division of labor and formal hierarchical authority make it impossible for egalitarianism, solidarity, and self-management to appear. Social relationships are structured from top to bottom. With this opinion, I reaffirm what I wrote above. Direct democracy is revealed as the only hypothesis for Solidarity Economy to emerge in contemporary societies as a process of socialization production and sociability leading to the development of solidarity, egalitarianism, and self-management.

Igor Valentim is an author deeply linked to research activity. Its sensitivity does not dissociate the observant subject from the observed subject. Researching with the method of cartography, formulated by Gilles Deleuze and Félix Guattari, implies experiencing and monitoring processes, eliminating methodologies that are limited to representing objects. As the author of this book states, at a given moment, cartography portrays daily life based on the experiences of the subjects. The researcher subject and the observed subject are affected and affect each other by their reason, intuition, and sensitivity.

Cartography is a very appropriate existential methodology for interpreting, explaining, and understanding the nature of solidarity economy. The researcher is constrained to feel, act, and think in a unique function of what he can see and experience in the real world. This real-world, however, needs to be encoded and decoded in the space-time of the subjects' experiences.

One of the important aspects of this book refers to the contextualization of the Solidarity Economy within the crisis of contemporary societies. It is a topic of extreme economic, social, political, cultural, and civilizational importance. It is not enough for us to state the crisis of state and market regulation. In addition to poverty and social exclusion, the environmental crisis affecting planet Earth, the levels of unemployment rates, and the precariousness of contractual ties indicate an unprecedented crisis of capitalism, surpassing in many respects the crisis of 1929.

In agreement, with Igor Valentim, first, we are facing a crisis of Western civilization. The gap between the real economy and the virtual economy is wide. The gap between the financial system and the economic, social, political, and cultural systems develops profoundly. The value of work and employment, as well as values, ethics, and morals, do not work in objective and subjective terms. Every human being is disposable as a commodity because it cannot be anything else as an object of purchase and sale.

Several factors are at the origin of the decay of Western civilization. Among them, I highlight ICT (Information and Communication Technologies). These are visible through computer science, nanotechnology, the internet, artificial intelligence, biotechnology, bioscience, technoscience, telematics, robotics, web languages, etc... Their complex and automatic mechanisms integrate an infinite amount of information, knowledge, and human energy. Let us say that in their complexity and abstraction, ICT embodies and streamlines a gigantic production, distribution, exchange, and consumption of analytical-symbolic goods and services. ICT have confined us to the immaterial domain of the virtual economy. In any case, it is important to understand the extent to which there are similarities and discrepancies between the real economy and the virtual economy.

One manifestation of the crisis caused by ICT lies in the fact that the flows of information, knowledge, and energy of the virtual economy are not properly coded and decoded, in a timely and appropriate manner, by the work production factor. The virtual economy being, in essence, an analytical-symbolic work, is different from the work that fundamental the real economy. The materiality and objectivity of the real economy, in its quantitative and qualitative aspects, is constituted by information and human knowledge, and the main function of the factor of production work lies in the expenditure of physical energy.

Let us say that to encode and decode ICT languages implies having cognitive and emotional abilities. These capacities may translate into the socialization of knowledge, information, and energy that are directly reported to the production, distribution, exchange, and consumption of analytical-symbolic goods and services. This power of the virtual economy - induced by ICT action - subverts the normative logic of the real economy. The logical result of this whole historical process is quite visible in the failure of many classical economic activities that emerged in the 19th and 20th centuries.

If we consider the structural effects of ICT in the context of the current crisis, we cannot stick exclusively to the negative effects of the virtual economy on the real economy. To work with ICT, it is essential to have cognitive and emotional abilities. Possessing these capabilities, all work production factors must, in a timely and appropriate manner, decode and encode the analytical-symbolic languages that permeate the work process.

As a global work organization process, we should refer to the social division of labor, the levels of formal hierarchical authority, the decision-making process, and the leadership process. The social division of labor specializes and delimits the action of the sensory organs of the work production factor, prohibiting a cognitive and emotional action in the sense of an interaction circumscribed to a free and autonomous stimulus-response.

Formal hierarchical authority structures the socialization of information, knowledge, and energy in the downward direction, from top to bottom. The freedom and autonomy of the sensory organs of the work production factor are frankly conditioned, especially concerning those who work at the base of the organizational pyramid.

The decision-making process, by its vertical essence, is the subject of a series of filtering and constraints from the top to the base of the organizational pyramid. As it is a process of socialization of information, knowledge, and energy directly related to a series of decisions, constraints emerge easily due to the hierarchical essence of these decisions and the limited margin of freedom and autonomy of the labor production factor.

ICT is fundamentally dedicated to the existence of formal leadership within the work organization. Formal leadership implies a type of hierarchical stimulus-response, of obedience between bosses and subordinates. Information, knowledge, and energy circulate from top to bottom. When informal leadership emerges the logic of formal leadership in the current work organization is subverted. The control of formal hierarchical authority and the behavioral rigidity of the social division of labor need to be abolished.

Informal leadership denies formal leadership because it is based on the spontaneity and informality of the action of the work production factor.

The examples I have focused on the structural effects of ICT on the organization of work help us understand the crisis that contemporary societies, in two main dimensions. First, the value of work suffers a great mischaracterization of its heuristic and instrumental value within capitalism. With ICT, much of the information, knowledge, and energy that was previously polarized to in the individual and collective action of the work production factor is suppressed or is the object of restructuring. Secondly, because there is a lot of ignorance, control, and rigidity in the current social division of labor, hierarchical authority, decision-making process, and leadership process, the productivity of the labor production factor is low and social conflict tends to develop.

The time has come to mention the importance of the skills and qualifications that the labor production factor must possess to adapt and react to ICT. Having skills and qualifications are two distinct but interdependent realities. Qualifications, in general cases, are modalities of certification and legitimation granted by companies, especially by institutions dedicated to this purpose. Competencies stem from the set of knowledge defined by a given profession or an individual. Competencies also imply the affirmation of these competencies by the factor of production work in the space-time of the work process.

ICT, in the concrete sense of the term, requires skills rather than qualifications, although these are part of a standard set of competencies. They are cognitive and emotional skills. They require that our sensory organs, especially at the level of hearing and vision, be in close harmony with the stimulus-response process leading to the socialization of energy, information, and knowledge. In this context, any work production factor that does not have the skills to perform the tasks required by ICT, either goes directly into unemployment or is considered disqualified.

The process of adaptation and the systematic reaction of the factor of production work to ICT generates four dichotomies that elucidate us about the nature of the crisis of contemporary societies. Firstly, ICT, because they integrate with their automatic mechanisms an immense living work in energy, information, and knowledge, in this way, dispense a substantial part of the living work inherent in the condition-function of the work factor. ICT, in these circumstances, structurally generates unemployment. The employment/unemployment dichotomy is irreversible. In this sense, as

ICT becomes more abstract and complex, and its automatic mechanisms become more sophisticated, living work unemployment in the condition-function of the work production factor is a reality immanent to the current crisis of capitalism.

Those who get jobs in the context of ICT and capitalism have adequate cognitive and emotional skills to integrate the process of production, distribution, exchange, and consumption of analytical-symbolic goods and services.

The qualifications of the work production factor registered at the level of the social division of labor, the formal hierarchical authority, the decision-making process, and the leadership process determine the place that each work production factor occupies in the pyramid of work organization. Thus, whoever occupies a place in space-time at the top of the work organization pyramid is considered a skilled worker. Otherwise, who is in the base of the pyramid of work organization production factor work is disqualified. To be qualified requires many cognitive and emotional skills, a lot of information and knowledge, and little energy. For the disqualified, a lot of energy, little information, and knowledge are required. The qualified/disqualified dichotomy evolves in the sense of employment/unemployment. Besides, the condition-function of disqualified translates into precarious situations of contractual binding.

Two more dichotomies emerge. Those who have jobs and qualify are doctors of social inclusion. Those who are unemployed and disqualified go through social exclusion. Social inclusion/social exclusion is an enhancer of social conflicts. When it reaches relevant proportions, it can give rise to radical social movements, forcing or demanding social, economic, political, and cultural changes.

Those who earn significant wage income and have a very reasonable standard of living, in most cases, are following the current social system. This situation occurs with the work production factor that has employment and is qualified. The same cannot be inferred from those who are unemployed, are disqualified, and have a precarious contractual relationship. These are often submerged by poverty. Slavery often accompanies this reality of misery and poverty. This wealth/poverty dichotomy is one of the most compelling manifestations of contemporary societies. The violence of the regulation of antinomies wealth/poverty does not overcome the contradictions and conflicts of the immense crisis that cross contemporary societies.

Contextualizing Solidarity Economy within contemporary societies, its epistemological and methodological approach is very recent. Its practical and theoretical significance has relevance, fundamentally, in Brazil and France, later extending to Portugal. Agreeing with Igor Valentim, Solidarity Economy has always been in continuous tension with the capitalist mode of production. While this model excelled in obtaining profit, competition, and competition determined by market rules, Solidarity Economy strives for a model of socialization based on solidarity, egalitarianism, and self-management.

As I have already explained, these assumptions of solidarity, egalitarianism, and self-management have their genesis in the mid-19th century in Western Europe. The experiences did not have the name of Solidarity Economy but were characterized as cooperatives, mutual relief associations, savings banks, etc. In most cases, they were alternatives to capitalism and socialism, especially when it is established in the USSR in Solidarity Economy, as theory and practice, appears in the mid-1990s of the 20th century, after May 1968 and the fall of the Berlin Wall in 1989.

A first major problem for Solidarity Economy is whether there is exclusively a tension with the capitalist mode of production or also with the socialist mode of production. The concepts of solidarity and egalitarianism inevitably lead us to this dilemma. What socialism is identified with Solidarity Economy? If it is not identified with any kind of socialist society, one may ask to what extent Solidarity Economy has a solid basis to be an alternative to the capitalist mode of production.

In his book, Igor Valentim analyzes the experiences of Solidarity Economy in Portugal. For the proper purposes, he sought examples of Solidarity Economy in mainland Portugal. Having not been able to find something that corresponded to the study he had carried out in Porto Alegre, Brazil, he was constrained to live the experiences of Solidarity Economy in the Azores. After several interviews with privileged informants in the context of the experiences that took place several years ago in this archipelago, it was possible to find an emblematic example through Megasil organization.

What is important, from now on, is the fact that Igor Valentim refuses to study/learn from the experiences that had been presented to him as a model of Solidarity Economy. The refusal to study certain companies, quite simply, resulted from the lack of processes of socialization and sociability conducive to the emergence of solidarity, egalitarianism, and self-management. It was this refusal that led him to Megasil.

Megasil's experience is notable for the persistence, motivation, and effort of those who work in it. Solidarity overlaps with egalitarianism and self-management. Since some of the women are physically disabled, this did not prevent their contribution to the final product from being extremely positive. The perpetuation of this experience, bearing in mind a situation of employment crisis in the region, reveals to us that Megasil approaches positively the theoretical and practical bases of Solidarity Economy.

Finally, in most companies, management is the opposite of self-management. Both in the aspects related to the social division of labor, as well as to formal hierarchical authority, as well as to the decision-making process and the leadership process, the assumptions of socialization and sociability of the exercise of power, and the execution of tasks are substantially different. The management model of capitalist companies implies an exercise of power and execution of tasks in the vertical direction, from top to bottom, with differentiated salaries, depending on the role of each in the organizational pyramid of the work organization. Democracy is representative and sometimes participatory. Igor Valentim criticizes certain organizations that adopt this management model: NGOs, unions, universities. When considering self-management as something different, he opines towards a kind of direct democracy that allows self-management, egalitarianism, and solidarity.

Dawn on the Azorean coast
São Miguel island, Azores
May 17, 2009
Photo by Igor Vinicius Lima Valentim

I
CONTEMPORARY CARTOGRAPHIES

We all live on the same planet Earth. We human beings alone are more than seven billion, not to mention the countless non-human forms of life, as important and constituent of ourselves as the environment in which we live. Thus, it is not an exaggeration to emphasize that **we share the same habitat.**

If today we can be aware of how many we are and how we are distributed around this planet, we are also able to know a little about the lives of many beings, as human as we are, spread across the globe. Differences in customs, habits, lifestyles, opportunities, values, senses: we live infinite differences intertwined.

From Rio de Janeiro to Lisbon, from Chittagong to Copenhagen, what ways do people find to survive? How do they give/build meaning to their experiences? We do not even have to make long trips. Walking inside a city like Rio de Janeiro, Brazil, with its approximately six million residents, in the geopolitical South, or walking through the streets of Copenhagen, Denmark, with approximately one million inhabitants and traditionally named as a reference for citizenship and development, multiple differences become clear.

It is noteworthy that the aforementioned differences are not found only when contrasting Rio with Copenhagen, or a rich country with a poor country, as they materialize within each country, state or city.

When walking through the streets of Copenhagen, for example, it is difficult not to be touched by certain details. Several young people sit on the edge of the trendy Nyhawn canal to enjoy yet another happy hour to the sound of instrumental music in the Danish capital. Among them, two people seek their survival by filling iron carts with metal cans and glass bottles. To drink a bottle of beer on-site, you pay more than 30 DKK (more than four Euros or ten Brazilian Reais). However, for those people to get the same thirty Danish crowns, they need to pick up and take more than fifty empty bottles of the same beer to a supermarket or a point of purchase for recyclable materials.

I observe more than differences: severe and numerous discrepancies, inequalities, that immediately call our sensibilities. Every day the gap is widening between those who enjoy the countless 'wonders' ready for consumption around the planet and those who are unable to have a minimally respectful life.

We build increasingly unfair societies. We cannot refrain from admitting that we live (and help to build) numerous injustices on a worldwide scale and that individual and collective human ways of life evolve towards progressive deterioration[1].

While millions of people live hungry around the world, and even in cities considered to be very wealthy, many people fail to recognize themselves in the social frameworks: crises of life models, sensitivity, models of social relationships, which exist not only in the poorest 'underdeveloped' countries but also in the masses of countries considered 'developed'[2].

Therefore, classifications such as rich/poor, developed/developing countries, are inaccurate and end up hiding growing social discrepancies, even in those countries considered rich or developed. Often the well-being of one place and the misery of another share the same city, the same neighborhood, the same geographical place.

In the documentary entitled 'Meeting with Milton Santos or the Global World Seen from the Side of Here', directed by Sílvio Tendler[3], quoting Josué de Castro in his 1961 text 'Geopolitics of Hunger', Brazilian geographer Milton Santos states that the world is divided into two groups: those who do not eat and those who do not sleep, for fear of the revolt of

---

1   GUATTARI, F. As três ecologias. Campinas: Papirus, 1990, p. 7.

2   GUATTARI, F.; ROLNIK, S. Micropolítica: cartografias do desejo. Petrópolis: Vozes, 2007, p. 218.

3   TENDLER, S. Encontro com Milton Santos ou O Mundo Global Visto do Lado de Cá. 2007.

those who do not eat. Nevertheless, classifications such as those mentioned fail to point out deep interconnections and interdependencies.

Polish sociologist Zygmunt Bauman[4] summarizes what happens brilliantly when he says that "there is no well-being in one place that is innocent of the misery of another". Modern societies have some advances that bring benefits to the lives of some, but, on the other hand, misery is the reality of a growing part of the world population, even with economic progress[5].

I agree with Roberto Freire[6] when he states that it is difficult to logically understand how humans may have become the predatory animal par excellence, the most irresponsible of all regarding his survival as a species. Félix Guattari[7] does not exaggerate when considering that "increasingly natural balances will depend on human interventions", including concerning the regulation of the relationships between oxygen, ozone, and carbon dioxide in the Earth's atmosphere.

In line with similar thinking, the Chilean biologist Humberto Maturana and Greta Verden-Zöller[8] affirm that we, human beings, "today live in a gift that occurs in the expansion of the human presence that is transforming the terrestrial biosphere into a human-centered homosexual or ecosystem". This is because "the human being considers himself the most developed, in addition to the most adapted and the strongest of all living beings", however, it took centuries for this evolution, with which man also became an "ecosystem manipulator"[9].

José Maria Carvalho Ferreira[10] considers that the biological and social perversions created by industrialization and urbanization processes have already reached their maximum limit: we live a model of "transformation of organic matter into inorganic matter" that generated an unsustainable situation regarding the environment and spatial planning.

This is felt, primarily, in the transformation, destruction, reduction

4   BAUMAN, Z. Vida Líquida. Rio de Janeiro: Jorge Zahar Ed., 2007, p. 6.

5   HANDY, C. A era do paradoxo. São Paulo: Makron Books, 1995.

6   FREIRE, R. A farsa ecológica. Rio de Janeiro: Guanabara Koogan, 1992.

7   GUATTARI, F., op. cit., p. 52.

8   MATURANA, H. R.; VERDEN-ZÖLLER, G. The origin of humanness in the biology of love. Exeter: Imprint Academic, 2008, p. 30.

9   FREIRE, R, op. cit., p. 42.

10   FERREIRA, J. M. C. Da impossibilidade de superar a actual crise do capitalismo. Utopia, n. 26, p. 7-16, julho/dezembro 2008, p. 9.

and massive extinction of the natural resources, water, and oxygen of the planet Earth, in the qualitative and quantitative gigantism of the exploration of the soil, mountains, rivers, seas, and forests that served and serve as materials raw materials for the production, distribution, exchange, and consumption of goods limited to the automobile, chemical, steel, oil, nuclear energy, iron, cement, glass, textile, real estate, transport, and agri-food sectors[11].

Just as people became commodities, so do every component of the 'natural kingdom', which must be manufactured and traded rampantly[12].

It is important to note that humanity's relations with socius and with 'nature' tend to deteriorate more and more, not only due to harmfulness and objective pollution. The very fact that we see the environments of which we are a part and in which we live as something external to us already gives clues to the bases on which we structure our ways of seeing, feeling, and thinking.

An important motivator of this situation is the existence of a fatalistic passivity. The situations we experience, even the most catastrophic ones, are usually accepted and treated naturally. **We are constantly led to believe that we can do nothing to change things as they are and that we are too small to build different modes of existence.**

However, we must make a significant effort not to notice the clear incapacity of contemporary societies, through their dominant logic, development, and so-called progress in promoting the minimum conditions necessary for most of the population to live.

Milton Santos considers, in the above-mentioned documentary, that never in the history of mankind we have had, as today, the technical and scientific conditions to live with dignity. Wherever we look we find a paradox. The continuous development of new technical and scientific means capable of solving dominant ecological problems is notorious - which include the very inability of humans to live harmoniously among themselves and with other living beings - but the incapacity of social forces is also evident and the subjective formations constituted in appropriating these means to make them operational[13], that is, to use them to effectively solve the mentioned problems.

---

11   Idem.

12   FREIRE, R, op. cit., p. 53.

13   GUATTARI, F, op. cit., p. 52.

We live under the hegemony of a capitalist logic which is founded on personal interests, private property, and profit; values that have been gradually transposed and insistently naturalized in all relational spheres of life on the planet. This logic is also based on technical and scientific development, the fallacy of economic development as a solution to all problems, the unrestricted accumulation of capital, and the commodification of all spheres of life: everything can be bought and everything is for sale.

The incentives for individualism, utilitarianism, and competition are noteworthy: for the enjoyment of some, the lives of many are destroyed, along with the very planet. Nardi[14] points out that "a solitary individualism is encouraged, in which each young person feels the sole responsibility for their survival and that of the family". We build and live in environments marked by competition, in which colleagues are transformed into opponents in the struggle for working and surviving.

Only one thing is treated as universal: the market, "a fantastic fabrication of wealth and misery"[15]. Félix Guattari[16] qualifies the current stage of capitalism as an Integrated World Capitalism (IWC), as it tends to decentralize its focuses of power from structures of production of goods and services to structures of production of subjectivities.

Therefore, capitalism as the dominant logic today is not linked exclusively to the production of goods and services, but it is itself a way of producing different logics and worlds. Values. Gilles Deleuze[17] portrays this well when he affirms that capitalism today is no longer directed towards production, often relegated to the periphery of the Third World and China, even in the complex forms of textiles, metallurgy or oil. We live in a capitalism that is not limited to buying raw materials and selling finished products, nor to buying finished products and assembling spare parts.

Naomi Klein addresses another aspect of contemporary capitalism and coined the expression "disaster capitalism" to name this logic that is now dominant: a logic that takes advantage of the public sphere in the wake of catastrophic events, treating disaster situations as opportunities to profit. Capitalism uses this "shock doctrine" as one of the main methods

---

14   NARDI, H. C. Ética, trabalho e subjetividade: trajetórias de vida no contexto das transformações do capitalismo contemporâneo. Porto Alegre: Editora da UFRGS, 2006, p. 191.

15   DELEUZE, G. Conversações. São Paulo: Ed. 34, 1992, p. 213.

16   GUATTARI, F, op. cit., p. 31.

17   DELEUZE, G, op. cit.

to advance corporate goals, "using moments of collective trauma to carry out radical social and economic engineering"[18].

In another passage of the same text, she clarifies how this doctrine works, analyzing that from a disastrous event such as a tsunami, terrorist attack, the breakdown of some market, among many others, part of the population goes into a collective state of shock and/or commotion. It is precisely this state of shock that capitalism uses as a market opportunity, such as the example of the Asian tsunami, from which thousands of fishermen were removed from their coastal homes and areas sold to major hotel chains[19].

This facet of capitalism mobilizes emotions and uses fear, apathy, and commotion as market opportunities. In this sense, it would not be a question of any conspiracy theory to consider that events of commotion and even some disasters can be enhanced and even articulated by states and private organizations, allied to the media as an important distributor of versions and meanings for the 'facts'.

To what extent are cuts in wages and pensions needed 'to save the country' when the role of the state should be to guaranteeing a better living condition for all? More and more governments appear to be run like banks and this idea is built, publicized, and accepted by many as natural.

Contemporary crises are not only at the level of explicit social relations, but also encompass religious, mythical, aesthetic formations: "it is a crisis of the modes of subjectivation, of the modes of organization and sociability", a crisis that at the same time it is worldwide, but "apprehended and mapped in different ways"[20].

The space-time of everyday life for individuals and groups is increasingly being capitalized on: "everything is sold and bought on the market of daily life: love, work, honor, dignity, justice, violence, crime, goods, and various consumption services, organs of the human organism, death"[21]. Today, the right to have rights (including the most basic ones) means having purchasing power, being a consumer[22]. And, to obtain the most basic means of survival, most of the world's population need a job.

---

18 KLEIN, N. The shock doctrine. The rise of disaster capitalism. London: Penguin Books, 2007, p. 8.

19 ibidem, p. 17.

20 GUATTARI, F.; ROLNIK, S., op. cit., p. 219.

21 FERREIRA, J. M. C., op. cit., p. 23.

22 NEGRI, A.; COCCO, G. GlobAL: biopoder e luta em uma América Latina globalizada. Rio de Janeiro: Record, 2005, p. 53.

The Centrality of Work-Employment

Work has long been considered a central entity and is treated today as our natural engine. As indicated by Viviane Forrester[23], deformed under the perverse form of employment, work founds Western civilization. It is no exaggeration to say that people are evaluated by society in general, to a large extent, according to the tasks they perform, what they produce, their supposed qualifications, and the organizations to which they belong (when they do).

It is by having a job that most people can find the means to obtain their survival. It is noticeable in the daily despair of many people around the planet the idea that to survive, they must be considered useful to society or "at least to the part that manages and dominates it: the economy"[24].

Being unemployed implies that the individual is no longer essential and/or necessary, "seeing himself exiled to the garbage dump of economic progress"[25]. This progress is reduced to doing equal jobs, with identical earnings, but with less staff and at a lower labor cost. As well explained by Robert Castel[26], those who do not have a job are treated as "useless to the world".

It is in the workplace that the rights of dignity and social respect continue to be obtained or lost[27]. The job market inspires and promotes division, placing a premium on competitive attitudes and causing collaboration and collective work to be suspended or ended as soon as its benefits are exhausted[28]: since competition replaces solidarity, individuals find themselves abandoned to their own - inadequate - resources[29].

It is difficult to disagree with Félix Guattari when he says that "the individual and collective ways of life evolve towards a progressive

---

23 FORRESTER, V. O horror econômico. São Paulo: Editora da Universidade Estadual Paulista, 1997, p. 7.

24 FORRESTER, V., op. cit., p. 13.

25 BAUMAN, Z. Confiança e medo na cidade. Lisboa: Relógio D'Água Editores, 2006, p. 20.

26 CASTEL, R. As metamorfoses da questão social. Petrópolis: Vozes, 1998, p. 496.

27 BAUMAN, Z. Amor líquido: sobre a fragilidade dos laços humanos. Rio de Janeiro: Jorge Zahar Ed., 2004, p. 36.

28 BAUMAN, Z. Vida Líquida. Rio de Janeiro: Jorge Zahar Ed., 2007, p. 2-3.

29 ibidem, p. 68.

deterioration"[30]. Contrary to the neoclassical thesis, unemployment and social discrepancies, considered market failures, are the necessary result of capitalist accumulation and competition, as well as of capitalist production relations, since capitalism is neither balanced nor tends to balance[31].

In the wake of competition as a beacon of human coexistence, unemployment takes on "a naturalized feature, an integral part of a Darwinian social life model, where it is understood that survival in the market is a process of natural selection"[32]. The term unemployed itself, which suggests a temporary state outside of normality, seems to deserve questioning since it is a long-term reality for large population groups around the world[33].

The prevailing belief that competition is fundamental and healthy for the development of people and societies is naturalized. With competition being accepted as something natural and human, more and more people are encouraged to trust their abilities, skills, and efforts, being equally treated as being solely responsible for their 'success' or 'failure'.

Getting a job is currently treated as an exclusive responsibility of each one. In Western countries, wage employment remains the dominant form under which capitalism exploits cooperation and the power of the invention of any subjectivities[34]. Maurizio Lazzarato considers that today unemployment and poverty "can no longer be qualified by the lack of work (of employment)"[35] since capitalism as the production of ways of life proves to be a force for the destruction of cooperation between brains and their conditions - including biological ones - of existence.

Michel Foucault already pointed out[36] that the art of punishment itself needs a technology of representation and that, therefore, companies can only be successful if they are inscribed in natural mechanics. We feel increasingly

---

30   GUATTARI, F., op cit., p. 7.

31   CARCHEDI, G. The social face of european capitalism. In: TITTENBRUN, J. (Ed.). Capitalism or Capitalisms? Szczecin: My Book, 2009. p. 44-77, p. 55.

32   GURGEL, C. A gerência do pensamento: gestão contemporânea e consciência neoliberal. São Paulo: Cortez, 2003, p. 119.

33   BAUMAN, Z. Confiança e medo na cidade. Lisboa: Relógio D'Água Editores, 2006.

34   LAZZARATO, M., op. cit., p. 88.

35   Ibidem, p. 150.

36   FOUCAULT, M. Vigiar e punir: nascimento da prisão. Petrópolis: Vozes, 2005, p. 87.

isolated and fragile, and this insecurity generated by unemployment is important for the internalization and naturalization of the dominant discourse of contemporary management and liberal ideals.

We live and build consumer societies, in which the predominant values relate to having, to the detriment of being. We cultivate values that emphasize competing, dominating, and discarding, in addition to the victory of the strongest and best prepared. This culture "does not offer conditions for human beings to see themselves internally, to question themselves about values. The tendency is to repeat models without asking yourself"[37].

We come to think that there are no alternatives outside what is presented and disseminated today as natural. We are sometimes permeated by a painful perception of impotence to cure the miseries we see.

Capitalism is not something external to us, but we build it daily, including through the values (solidarity, individualism, competition, greed, love, among many others) that we cultivate in our daily attitudes.

I am inspired by Maturana and Verden-Zöller's conception of value, who consider that "values are abstractions that we make about our operation as social beings"[38] and that they do not exist in themselves. However, values can be understood as declarations of the desired or intended ways of human coexistence that we do out of concern for the other. Based on this, it is possible to understand that values need to be cultivated as aspects of our living so to become spontaneous. Capitalist logic seeks to naturalize in us only certain values, to the detriment of others.

The creation of possible worlds become the objects of capitalist appropriation[39]. The company that produces a service or a commodity creates a world since products and services need to be inserted in the souls and bodies of workers and consumers: "in contemporary capitalism, the company does not exist outside the producer and the consumer who represent"[40]. The targets are our hearts, intellects, wills, and dispositions[41].

With the insertion of products and services in people's values, desires, and needs, the incessant search for capitalist profit at any price becomes more and more concrete and natural. And the issue is not restricted to products

37   ZANETI, I. As sobras da modernidade. Porto Alegre, 2006, p. 82.

38   MATURANA, H. R.; VERDEN-ZÖLLER, G., op. cit., p. 135.

39   LAZZARATO, M., op. cit., p. 145.

40   Ibidem, p. 99.

41   FOUCAULT, M., op. cit., p. 18.

and services. "Work acts directly on affects; it produces subjectivity; it produces society; it produces life"[42]. Suely Rolnik makes an important contribution when she says that

> it is not only from biological life that capitalism is interested [...] but also from subjective life, in which the feeling of self is produced and territories of existence are configured[43].

But what do I mean when I talk about subjectivity?

Work, Values, and Subjectivity

Reflecting about the connections between work and subjectivity implies understanding the processes through which work experiences stimulate and constitute ways of acting, thinking, and feeling. I understand subjectivity inspired by Michel Foucault as "how the subject experiences himself in real games"[44]. Subjectivity is related to the processes by which these experiences occur[45].

When I deal with subjectivity I am also dealing with the different possibilities of creation and invention of other ways of producing, working, and living.

In contemporary capitalism, subjectivity is a central theme, since this logic's essential production concerns behaviors, perceptions, sensitivities, social relations, imaginary ghosts, among many other aspects. In this sense, the production of goods and commodities has a complementary role to the main core of capitalism, constituted by the management of current and potential forms of human life in its different spheres.

Some economists have realized, in recent years, that the nature of contemporary work demands more and more ingredients such as the production of bonds, reciprocal affectation and collective intelligence,

---

42   HARDT, M. O trabalho afetivo. In: PELBART, P. P.; COSTA, R. D. (Ed.). O Reencantamento do concreto. Cadernos de Subjetividade. São Paulo: Editora Hucitec, 2003. p. 143-157, p. 156.

43   ROLNIK, S. Despachos no museu: sabe-se lá o que vai acontecer. In: FONSECA, T. M. G.; KIRST, P. G. (Ed.). Cartografias e devires: a construção do presente. Porto Alegre: Editora da UFRGS, 2003. p. 207-218, p. 207.

44   FOUCAULT, M. La creación de modos de vidaEstética, ética y hermenéutica. Barcelona: Paidós, 1999, p. 16.

45   TITTONI, J. Subjetivação e trabalho: reflexões sobre a Economia Solidária. In: VIII Congresso Luso-Afro Brasileiro de Ciências Sociais, setembro 2004, Coimbra. Centro de Estudos Sociais, 2004, p. 5.

understood as the life power of a collective, created precisely from of the living force that is subjectivity[46]. Gilles Deleuze puts the theme brilliantly when he says that "subjectification is the production of ways of existence or lifestyles"[47]. Therefore, the subjectivation processes are constituted in the different forms through which the subjects are constructed and are constructed from their life experiences[48].

The subject is not something given, which we find ready, like a déjà-la, something in the domain of a supposed human nature or essence. On the contrary, subjectivity has a 'machinic' nature[49], that is, it is manufactured, modeled, received, consumed.

Subjectivity can be understood in terms of its processual aspects, its permanent movements of becoming, of what will come to be constituted from exchanges with what is outside its pores: "subjectivity is, then, something always built, manufactured, produced in meetings"[50], as well as subjectivity-building processes can be captured by certain ways of doing since they are always in relation to a web of knowledge and strategies.

There are several subjectivity-producing 'machines', such as companies and the media, to name just two examples. But what is most interesting to emphasize at this point of the work is that within the capitalist logic, as it appears today, the production of subjectivity is industrial and occurs on a large scale. In other words, components are manufactured on an international scale aimed at building ways of being, thinking, acting, and feeling.

Gilles Deleuze makes an important point when he postulates that the processes of subjectivation are not about 'private life', but about the operation by which individuals or communities are constituted as subjects, apart from the constituted knowledge and the established powers[51].

These processes of subjectivation - or production of subjectivities - occur

---

46   PELBART, P. P. Da função política do tédio e da alegria. In: FONSECA, T. M. G.; KIRST, P. G. (Ed.). Cartografias e devires: a construção do presente. Porto Alegre: Editora da UFRGS, 2003. p. 69-78, p. 73.

47   DELEUZE, G., op. cit., p. 142.

48   NARDI, H. C., op. cit., p. 133.

49   GUATTARI, F.; ROLNIK, S., op. cit., p. 33.

50   GIACOMEL, A. E. et al. Trabalho e contemporaneidade. o trabalho tornado vida. In: FONSECA, T. M. G.; KIRST, P. G. (Ed.). Cartografias e devires: a construção do presente. Porto Alegre: Editora da UFRGS, 2003. p. 137-148, p. 143.

51   DELEUZE, G., op. cit., p. 188-189.

since childhood and the child's entry into the world of dominant languages and imaginary and technical models, in which he must be inserted[52]. The production of subjectivity is the raw material of all production, but, within the contemporary capitalist logic, representations are injected into mothers and children, as part of the subjective production process[53].

Contemporary capitalist logic, therefore, acts in actions, gestures, feelings, thoughts, affections, in all our perceptions, memories and so many other instances. Capitalism has been manufacturing, from an early age, how we speak, learn, listen, love. Nevertheless, this logic contributes to the production and reproduction of the relationships we establish with the body, with food, with 'nature', with what we consider past, present, and future. In short, "it fabricates the relationship of man with the world and with himself"[54], causing us to create and reinforce the idea that things 'are like this', that the world 'is like this' and, above all, that there is no way to organize life in other ways.

We live and build societies whose main objective is limited to the production and accumulation of capital. It is not even easy to notice that it is increasingly more difficult to create and build diverse ways of living, feeling, and thinking. Our 'freedom' is exercised exclusively to choose from among the possibilities that others have instituted and conceived: "we are left without the right to participate in the construction of worlds, to formulate problems and invent solutions, unless within already established alternatives"[55]. This is a condition for forming a solid workforce and social control, which is why "a powerful complex of collective equipment is being installed that centralizes the distribution of meanings and values"[56], which are progressively taken by us as a reference and internalized as our own.

In worlds in which work occupies a central place for people's survival, and they are led to believe that it is available almost exclusively in large companies, it is even considered a privilege to be employed by some company large multinational private company.

Privilege remains the supreme virtue in people's search for the promised land of success: "make yourself a best seller or at least a guaranteed one,

---

52   GUATTARI, F.; ROLNIK, S., op. cit., p. 49.

53   Ibidem, p. 36.

54   Ibidem, p. 51.

55   LAZZARATO, M., op. cit., p. 101-102.

56   ROLNIK, S., op. cit., p. 91-92.

always inside and, if possible, on top"[57]. For this, a large part of the population spares no effort: from physical exercises, through alternative treatments and weight loss programs, to surgical interventions for aesthetic purposes.

Not even professors are immune to this. It seems more and more common and natural that the good teacher is precisely the one who does best in the competitive rankings among professional colleagues. To be good it is necessary to publish more, to be recognized as the best, and preferably before other peers. It does not matter how this occurs: only the result matters.

The most symptomatic is that this type of judgment is not made only by government entities or funding agencies: every day more and more teachers internalize these competitive values as natural and start to judge themselves based on these values.

It is interesting to notice how blaming is a capitalist function[58] and has great importance in the way we live today. We are always faced with reference images (successful man, successful entrepreneur, dedicated husband, good father, among many others) from which we question who we are, how we will be classified by society, and even if we are good enough.

We are always at fault, always needy, always wanting something we have not yet achieved: always living in terms of images, goals, and objectives that we build mainly from images valued by the media.

Every day it seems more difficult to invent ways that question this direction and build other ways of living. To daily question the dominant values, and/or to cultivate different ones requires a redoubled effort. We are often encouraged to think that the best thing to do is to keep quiet and internalize the values that others consider to be the most desirable for us.

Therefore, more than just an economic subjection, we speak of a subjective subjection, according to which more and more values, meanings, goals, objectives, behaviors, ways of perceiving, feeling, seeing and acting business are naturalized and internalized as of population, becoming part of their desires.

I consider desire, within this work, as "all forms of the will to live, the will to create, the will to love, the will to invent another society, another perception of the world, other value systems"[59]. It should be noted that

---

57   ROLNIK, S., op. cit., p. 184.

58   GUATTARI, F.; ROLNIK, S., op. cit., p. 49.

59   GUATTARI, F.; ROLNIK, S., op. cit., p. 260-261.

although according to contemporary capitalism , desire is seen as related to pleasure and dissociated from the 'real' and 'effective', I seek inspiration in this aforementioned conception to question other ways of seeing and acting, about ways of fabricating other realities and other references.

It is through desires that the worlds are built: "there is no society that is not made of investments of desire in this or that direction, with this or that strategy"[60]; the desire corresponds to the design of new configurations in the social field, being the very production of the social reality. The desire is always the mode of production of something, the desire is always the way of building something[61].

But where does capitalist logic look for desires to go? How are they being built? All people are being converted into a workforce, fearing that they will not be able to obtain the means for more immediate survival, as they have less and less stable jobs. And each time you change jobs, you change references as well. People are, as never before, exposed to encounters, affecting, and being affected by all sides and in all ways, to de-territorialize themselves.

The process called by Suely Rolnik of deterritorialization occurs when the set of the existential territory of each person or group reorganizes itself, in a process in which the gestures, ways, procedures, facial expressions, and words become obsolete. In a world in which this process starts to happen with increasing speed, people start having to dedicate their time and money to try to manage it: "they can barely get dressed on one side and, on the other, they are already mess up entirely"[62].

All social is produced with the help of a multiplicity of people, who act on each other, propagating bodily and mental habits. If on the one hand, the development of this massive capitalist subjectivity brings a series of problems and dangers to humanity, on the other hand, it brings immense possibilities for deviation and appropriation.

Social affronts are no longer just of an economic nature, but also among the different ways in which individuals and groups understand to live their existence[63]. Therefore, the fight is no longer restricted to the political economy but focused on the subjective economy.

---

60   ROLNIK, S., op. cit., p. 58.

61   GUATTARI, F.; ROLNIK, S., op. cit., p. 260-261.

62   ROLNIK, S., op. cit., p. 87-88.

63   GUATTARI, F.; ROLNIK, S., op. cit., p. 53.

It is urgent to carry out valuation instruments based on existential productions that cannot be determined only by an expected profit. The notion of collective interest must encompass initiatives that, although they do not bring a 'return' in the short term, bring enrichment to humanity, and build different existential values.

This promotion of existential values and values of desire will not present itself as a global alternative, constituted once and for all, but will result from a generalized displacement of current value systems and the appearance of new valuation poles[64].

If it seems increasingly clear that we need a major reconstruction of social mechanisms that is not only about elite reforms, bureaucratic or legal programs, but also about building and promoting innovative practices focused on respecting the singularities that acquire autonomy and at the same time articulate with the rest of society[65].

Revolts are rarely treated as something positive, but they represent a movement of people who are no longer willing to endure certain situations and/or certain servitude. To revolt is necessary to break with what you can no longer bear. To revolt is to inflict distortions on the clichés[66]: "revolt is the passionate claim of essential value to man"[67]. And it is precisely this that can preserve us from the contamination of the absurd, constituting the source of our being and founding the value of human existence.

Although in numerical minorities, there are initiatives that seem to build different ways of working and producing; that seem to be based on different values from those that are dominant today; and that show signs of seeking to value diagrams of different references. Finally, they seem to be moving in other directions, posing problems that concern not only themselves but the whole of society.

---

64 GUATTARI, F., op. cit., p. 51.

65 GUATTARI, F., op. cit., p. 43-44.

66 KRISTEVA, J. Sentido e contra-senso da revolta: poderes e limites da psicanálise. Rio de Janeiro: Rocco, 2000.

67 CHAGAS, W. Mundo e contramundo. Porto Alegre: Editora da UFRGS, 1972, p. 69.

St. Iria Viewpoint
View of São Miguel island, Azores
May 16, 2009
Photo by Igor Vinicius Lima Valentim

II

AN EXPERIENTIAL CONSTRUCTION OF RESEARCH

This book is not just a closed product, but mainly a narrative linked to processes, experiences, experiments. Therefore, it is important to warn, right now, that I seek to share not only the result of research but paths and deviations built collectively, by me and all those with whom I have met over the past few years.

I strive to make this **with and not about** people and organizations. I present many of the paths and stories that made it possible, helped to build, and are effectively part of the research undertaken.

The experiences narrated here changed me as a researcher and as a human being and I also seek to share these changes on the pages that constitute this work.

I was born and lived until I was 23 in Rio de Janeiro, Brazil. I spent almost five years to get a bachelor's degree in Management in May 2003 from the Federal University of Rio de Janeiro (UFRJ). Until then, I had always lived in the same city, and I felt the need to breathe new air, listen to new stories, meet people in different places.

More than that, I felt uneasy, especially in the last two years of the program, when I saw two faces of what seemed to be the same phenomenon. On the one hand, having worked in an investment bank, a consulting company, the financial department of a computer enterprise, and in a language learning school, it was clear that exploration in and through work was a naked reality. On the other hand, what distressed me most was to see that almost all of my university classmates were doing endless overtime hours (many unpaid), and being absent and/or late in many classes, considered this type of policy to be natural: they aimed to grow within the companies in which they were working, in the form of employment or internship. They dreamed of being promoted or hired and thought that the university could wait forever since the important was to live and breathe 24/7 what the corporations expected of them.

During the five-year program, I was disciplined in a curriculum with courses related to financial, accounting, marketing, and human resources perspectives of management. The contents were all linked to companies that had profit as their primary and most natural objective. All other aspects of an organization, including people, were treated as resources. And all other types of companies and enterprises were simply non-existent during these five years.

I had the impression that everyone's participation was encouraged only in official organizational speeches and in situations where there was no intention of questioning organizations, their purposes, and the status quo.

It seemed to me that equality, solidarity, cooperation, and justice were beautiful words in business pamphlets and people management manuals, but of dubious operation, considering that the organizational profits were far from being shared equally by all and that wages seemed increasingly discrepant.

Many people earned low or very low wages while very few earned very high salaries and bonuses. Competition, the understanding of the other as an adversary or even an enemy, the treatment of cooperation and partnerships in a utilitarian and temporary way - only when they make a profit - were aspects of ways of life that were stimulated, cultivated and experienced in daily activities, both in the companies where I had worked and also inside the public university where I studied.

It distressed me to see that, in a federal, public, tuition-free university like UFRJ, a Management student had contact with nothing or almost nothing of critical content. The institution did not have, in this undergraduate program, any line of critical training for future managers.

Teaching/learning relationships took place all within the institution's walls, except for the requirement of a 3-month supervised internship. I had no contact with the possibility of participating in service-learning initiatives, academic monitoring, or scientific initiation projects. There did not seem to be any concerns about the impacts and consequences of the content taught to people and societies more broadly, except for the isolated initiatives of a few professors.

Administrative theories, management tools, and policies aimed at the administration of organizations and of human life itself were taught without even emphasizing the political character they carry and whose interests they seek to serve.

At the same time, political aspects were treated as matters exclusive to political parties, while linked to negative stigma and corruption. Thus, it loses its original conceptual characteristic: 'political', from the Greek *politikós*, concerns everything that has to do with what is public and, therefore, with the organization of life in society.

I was intrigued to see that the most diverse disciplines were taught as possessing an apolitical character, even though they stimulated the (re)production of pre-elaborated techniques, tools, behaviors, and ways of thinking.

How could values, such as competition, individualism, ambition, and the primacy of finance over all the rest, be stimulated and naturalized in a public university? Progressively, without reflecting much on what consequences they may have, these values are appropriated by many of us and virtually treated as necessary for those 'who wish to win'. In other words, these values and principles are expanded not only for the management of companies but for all areas/dimensions of our lives.

Actions and attitudes that go in other directions, guided by different values from those mentioned above, tend to be understood as naive, romantic, crazy, or even criminal. Others should only serve as long as they help to enhance their income and interests: utilitarianism in relationships.

It is rare to see incentives for collective mobilization, forms of management that encourage values such as cooperation, solidarity, and egalitarianism.

I had never heard of Solidarity Economy, associations, cooperativism, or even self-management. In other words, the management that I had learned until then in a public university and my jobs were performed in a single way - heterogeneous - and focused solely and exclusively on profit, even though disguised in the most diverse, beautiful, supposedly neutral, apolitical and compelling business management models, philosophies and tools.

But some initiatives do not seem to have profit as their primary objective, among which are some associations and cooperatives, named as belonging to Solidarity Economy (SE).

These collective organizations were said to seek values such as self-management, egalitarianism, and the primacy of the human over the financial. It was necessary to seek them, listen to them, live them.

Moving to Porto Alegre: experiencing another management

In January 2004, I drove 1,561km (almost 1,000 miles) towards the south of Brazil to live in Porto Alegre and get a master's degree in Management at the Federal University of Rio Grande do Sul (UFRGS).

Some friends said that I was crazy to think about taking a master's degree and to live with a scholarship: "will you be eating bread with mortadella[1] for two years instead of making more money on other jobs?", a colleague asked me.

The scholarship stipend I received at that time during 24 months was higher than the salary many people earned in their jobs, and although it did not allow me any kind of luxury, I could live with simplicity and dignity, doing what I wanted and believed. Besides, I considered myself a simple person and I did not have a wealthy family, but one with values that I greatly admired. I faced the challenge of the unknown and the unpredictable in favor of what affected and moved myself.

One of the biggest motivators of my move to Porto Alegre had been precisely a set of feelings related to all these experiences that had affected me during my graduation in Rio de Janeiro. I felt uneasy about the naturalness with which most people seemed to face the situations I had previously described.

I arrived in Porto Alegre at the beginning of 2004: a total stranger since I did not know anyone in the state capital further south of Brazil.

During the first month of the master's program, I sought to inform myself about the projects and research in progress at the UFRGS Management School (MS). It was then that I started to read several articles on the theme of Solidarity Economy (SE), self-managed organizations supposedly guided

---

1   Alluding to the financial difficulties that I would face living only with the scholarship's monthly stipend for master's students, financed by the Brazilian federal government.

by values such as solidarity and egalitarianism, different from those that constituted themselves as dominant and that distressed me so much.

In April of the same year, I started to sketch, together with a classmate, the lines for the first edition of an extension project that would involve the work of MS students in associations and cooperatives of Solidary Economy in Porto Alegre region. This project, entitled Solidary Residence, is presented in more detail in another work, published in 2006[2].

With my involvement in the construction of the first edition of the Solidary Residence in the state of Rio Grande do Sul, I encountered academic productions/publications and could know the daily life of some SE organizations. I participated as one of the three project coordinators and at the same time as a 'resident'. In my first task, I had the opportunity to meet several associations and cooperatives. In the second, together with Beatriz, another colleague, I was able to strengthen and deepen ties with one of these organizations.

One of the objectives as a participant in the Solidary Residence was to build a project together with the members of the associations, based on their demands. These were not always clear, and we had the intention, as residents, that they should be built collectively, and not based on suggestions from 'the university students'.

I started to build a story that would prove to be much deeper than a simple work with the Association of Waste Pickers of Recyclable Materials for the Rights of Homeless People (ACMDMR), constituted from the collective mobilization of then homeless people, in a struggle for better conditions of life and work.

We felt that if ACMDMR members used some administrative tools, the result of the collective work could be improved. But, on the other hand, we were fully aware of the risk that this 'import' of concepts and tools from traditional management could bring to the values and organization of the association.

The pompous theories, models, and management tools proved to be incompatible with the position of an association that did not seek profit as a major objective and that apparently fought for relations based on equality among its members.

The fallacy of the superiority of academic knowledge was

2   CARRION, R. M.; VALENTIM, I. V. L.; HELLWIG, R. C. (Orgs.). Residência Solidária UFRGS: vivência de universitários com o desenvolvimento de uma tecnologia social. Porto Alegre: Editora da UFRGS, 2006.

clear. Management theories and techniques were inadequate to contribute to the administration and the consolidation of an association based on principles different from the capitalist ones.

It was necessary to seek the construction of new collective knowledge. Not at the University or by the university students, but between our knowledge and theirs, without the superiority of one over the other.

To accomplish this task, it was also essential to discover what goals people had, what values they experienced in the relationships they built, what dreams they had, what life stories they carried, as well as marks left by victories, defeats, joys, and sadness.

It proved to be important to live the organization together with these people, as well as to sharpen my sensitivity with the meanings acquired by the work and life that materialized there.

I spent more than eighteen months going to the ACMDMR weekly. Strangeness and learning. Discomfort. Happiness. Joy. I was left with many unanswered questions. One of these questions was related to the meanings that the concept 'Solidarity Economy' acquired in other contexts, other regions, other countries, other organizations, considering that until I arrived at ACMDMR, its members did not know the concept.

There was already a discussion about Solidarity Economy in Brazil and other countries such as France and Canada since the mid-1990s. Since the 2000s, I could notice an increase in research and publications on the subject, both in Brazil, Latin American, and some French-speaking countries.

However, I was struck by the fact that in Portugal, a country responsible for the colonization of extensive areas of Brazilian territory, had also been discussing Solidarity Economy, especially since 2003, with the publications of Boaventura de Sousa Santos[3] - based on his presence in several editions of the World Social Forum - and Rogério Roque Amaro[4]. It surprised me because the Portuguese Constitution mentions and provides public policies for the Social Economy, representing another conceptual body, different from the Solidarity Economy.

None of the Portuguese publications that dealt with Solidarity Economy in Portugal that I could find brought field reports, presentations

---

3   SANTOS, B. D. S. (Ed.). Produzir para viver: os caminhos da produção não capitalista. Lisboa: Edições Afrontamento, 2003.

4   AMARO, R. R. Reflexões sobre a economia solidária. In: Actas do Congresso internacional de economia solidária, 29-30 sep 2005, Ponta Delgada. Centro de estudos de economia solidária do atlântico, 2005, p. 17-29.

of associations and/or cooperatives, or in-depth investigations carried out with SE organizations on Portuguese soil.

I seek the new. Invention. The potential. I was interested in finding organizations that were not necessarily created 'top to bottom'. Where to find, in Portugal, experiences of collective mobilization of people who fight for values such as egalitarianism, solidarity, and self-management in their organizations? Organizations in which the members are associated, members, owners, and in which they actively participate. Organizations that are not designed and thought by some and built daily and executed by others and in which values such as those mentioned in interpersonal relationships are pulsating. Organizations that represent alternatives in the construction of other worlds.

Methodological aspects

There are no right or wrong methods, false or true, in research development. The choice of the method is made according to research objectives, principles, and expectations. In other words, the method is a choice made with the research and during its development, to enhance it.

It was precisely in the course of experiences that the work began to take shape and that the research problems, as well as its objectives, were built. So I agree with the words of Virginia Kastrup[5] when she says that "one enters the field without knowing the target to be pursued; it will appear in a more or less unpredictable way, without us knowing where it is".

Several reasons lead me to carry out this work. Among them, it is important to highlight my interest in how people build their existence, as well as what types of societies these modes imply.

Academics[6] should question and even deconstruct what seems to represent, in the speech of many, the nature of people and things: modes of existence are not unique, natural, or inevitable.

Things (including ways of living) also are not pre-existing and independent

---

5   KASTRUP, V. O funcionamento da atenção no trabalho do cartógrafo. In: PASSOS, E. et al (Ed.). Pistas do método da cartografia: pesquisa-intervenção e produção de subjetividade. Porto Alegre: Sulina, 2009, p. 32-51.

6   The term refers, in the scope of this work, to professors, researchers, master's students, doctoral students, undergraduate students and all those who, directly, contribute to the construction of what is considered as science, with special attention to those who, from working at Academia, get the means to survive.

of every person's gaze: there is no scientific objectivity, neutrality in relationships, and, therefore, analytical neutrality[7].

Cartesian legacy[8],[9] differentiates the outside world from the inside world, founding scientific neutrality. Traditional rules of a method, called scientific, were created in which the subject-researcher and object-researched occupy fixed places, hoping that there are neutrality and detachment from history, the social environment, and the body itself[10].

But researchers configure themselves in what they can see and experience. We are always operating as observers and, therefore, what we explain is what we experience, that is, what we distinguish as events directly or indirectly linked to us[11]. What we approach in the research are experiences, since the behavior is not something given, but a series of events that happen between interactions.

This book can be understood as a cartographic exercise inspired by Suely Rolnik[12],[13],[14]. According to her, a cartography is "a drawing that accompanies and is made at the same time as the landscape transformation movements"[15] occur, seeking to capture

---

7   GUATTARI, F.; ROLNIK, S. Micropolítica: cartografias do desejo. Petrópolis: Vozes, 2007, p. 37.

8   DESCARTES, R. A discourse of a method for the well guiding of reason, and the discovery of truth in the sciences. London: Printed by Thomas Newcombe, 1649. Available at: http://gateway.proquest.com/openurl?ctx_ver=Z39.88-2003&res_id=xri:eebo&rft_val_fmt=&rft_id=xri:eebo:image:54569. Accessed on: 13 mar 2008.

9   DESCARTES, R. Les principes de la philosophie. In: ADAM, C.; TANNERY, P. (Ed.). Oeuvres de Descartes. Paris: Tomo IX-2, 1971.

10   KIRST, P. G. et al. Conhecimento e cartografia: tempestade de possíveis. In: FONSECA, T. M. G.; KIRST, P. G. (Ed.). Cartografias e devires: a construção do presente. Porto Alegre: Editora da UFRGS, 2003, p. 91-101, p. 96.

11   MATURANA, H. R.; VERDEN-ZÖLLER, G. The origin of humanness in the biology of love. Exeter: Imprint Academic, 2008, p. 15-16.

12   ROLNIK, S. Cartografia ou de como pensar com o corpo vibrátil. Núcleo de Estudos e Pesquisas da Subjetividade da PUC/SP, 1987.

13   ROLNIK, S. Pensamento, corpo e devir. Uma perspectiva ético/estético/política no trabalho acadêmico. Cadernos de Subjetividade PUC/SP, v. 1, n. 2, p. 241-251, sep 1993.

14   ROLNIK, S. Cartografia sentimental: transformações contemporâneas do desejo. Porto Alegre: Sulina; Editora da UFRGS, 2006.

15   ROLNIK, S. Cartografia ou de como pensar com o corpo vibrátil. Núcleo de Estudos e Pesquisas da Subjetividade da PUC/SP, 1987.

intensities and transformations in the terrain[16]. Meanwhile, the map represents a static whole, déjà-là.

Cartography is a method formulated by Gilles Deleuze and Félix Guattari[17] which seeks to monitor processes, and not to represent objects. It supposes an attempt to portray the daily life from the constituent marks that cross the subjects' experience[18]. Therefore, alliances between reason, intuition, and sensitivity, life, and knowledge are summoned, invoking the complexity and unlimited possibilities of expression, regarding both the world and the subjects[19].

It is worth mentioning that in encounters we have not only the 'object' but also the researcher is no longer the same: it is when we let ourselves be affected and redesigned by others who visit us[20], often settling in and becoming part of ourselves, that we build what I propose here.

Being a narrative and an explanation of sensations, cartography is produced through concepts, testimonies, conversations, confessions, commitments, and many other things. Concepts can never be separated from sensations since they are "their letters, their records or their vibrations"[21] and are present in everything that refers to existing and experiencing.

What could be called a description, based on these concepts, can be called existential production, no longer dissociating subject and object: "cartography aims to capture the moment of the meeting of the researcher's movements with the movements of the research territory. It is the encounter that is registered and not its objects"[22].

It is not my objective to demonstrate the veracity of propositions and/ or hypotheses, but rather to do science by paying attention to the marks of

16   KIRST, P. G. et al., op. cit, p. 92.

17   DELEUZE, G.; GUATTARI, F. Mil Platôs. Rio de Janeiro: Ed. 34 Letras, 1995.

18   REPPOLD, C. R. et al. O trabalho como dispositivo de subjetivação, hierarquia e controle no poder judiciário: um estudo de caso. In: FONSECA, T. M. G.; FRANCISCO, D. J. (Ed.). Formas de ser e habitar a contemporaneidade. Porto Alegre: Editora da UFRGS, 2000. p. 129-136, p. 130.

19   FONSECA, T. M. G.; KIRST, P. G. Cartografias e devires: a construção do presente. Porto Alegre: Editora da UFRGS, 2003, p. 12.

20   MAIRESSE, D. Cartografia: do método à arte de fazer pesquisa. In: FONSECA, T. M. G.; KIRST, P. G. (Ed.). Cartografias e devires: a construção do presente. Porto Alegre: Editora da UFRGS, 2003. p. 259-271, p. 260.

21   KIRST, P. G. et al., op. cit., p. 98.

22   Idem, p. 100.

encounters and the feelings and instabilities that cross the coexistence of the research development processes, that is, affections.

Affections are produced through bodies' encounters when they invoke us as the capacity to affect and be affected and it is not known in advance what affects they are capable of[23]. The very word 'affect' designates the effect of the action of one body on another, in its encounter[24].

It is precisely the power to affect and to be affected that determines the quality of what can be called an encounter, in which the freedom of a body is defined as the power to update its affections, to become their cause and source[25]. Affecting and being affected are, therefore, synonymous with living.

The thought is a kind of cartography whose raw material consists of the marks produced in encounters[26]. Mapping, for knowledge, means marking the moment of a glance, leaving aside sacred truths[27], since all knowledge refers to an effect of the contingencies that engendered it.

In a cartography, cartographers see themselves as integral parts of the investigation and witness their movements of knowing[28]. Therefore, once again I consider that there is no neutrality since it is precisely in encounters, with proximity, and in moments of coexistence that the work is carried out and that life gains contours.

Cartography appears as a principle "entirely focused on experimentations anchored in reality"[29]. There is not a single meaning to experiences. Reality presents itself "as a moving map", in such a way that everything that looks like 'the same' is just a concentrate of knowledge and power[30]. It is precisely by allowing oneself to dream from the intensities

---

23   DELEUZE, G. Francis Bacon: la lógica de la sensación. Madrid: Arena Libros, 2002.

24   ROLNIK, S. Cartografia sentimental: transformações contemporâneas do desejo. Porto Alegre: Sulina; Editora da UFRGS, 2006, p. 57.

25   ENGELMAN, S. Trabalho e loucura: uma biopolítica dos afetos. Porto Alegre: Sulina; Editora da UFRGS, 2006, p. 136.

26   ROLNIK, S. A dama de negro. Núcleo de Estudos e Pesquisas da Subjetividade da PUC/SP, 1993, p. 4.

27   FONSECA, T. M. G.; KIRST, P. G., op. cit., p. 11.

28   KIRST, P. G. et al., op. cit., p. 96.

29   DELEUZE, G.; GUATTARI, F., op. cit., p. 21.

30   PASSOS, E. et al. Apresentação. In: PASSOS, E. et al (Ed.). Pistas do método da cartografia: pesquisa-intervenção e produção de subjetividade. Porto Alegre: Sulina, 2009, p. 7-16, p. 10.

experienced in encounters that the social reality is produced: it seems "difficult and even inconceivable to separate a material field from a field of representation"[31].

The cartographer's profile is composed of a kind of sensitivity that he seeks to make prevail in his work: a mixture of his eye with, simultaneously, his vibrating body[32].

Cartographies are being designed while territories are taking shape: one cannot exist without the other. It is not possible to establish a linear path to reach an end when making a cartography: it is always "an ad hoc method"[33]. The problem, for the cartographer, is not that of false/true, nor that of theoretical/empirical[34]. Therefore, this book aims to portray experiences in the constitution of existential territories, in the analysis of the constitution of desires that happens in encounters.

Research requires dealing with territories that, in principle, the researcher/cartographer does not inhabit. No ready data *déjà-là*, waiting to be collected for further analysis, but an investigation that collectively builds knowledge in encounters between those involved and in the contexts of which the researcher is part. Thus, in a cartography, there is nothing to be described at the first moment to be analyzed *a posteriori*.

I lived in Lisbon and the Autonomous Region of the Azores, for a total period of almost two years, beginning in late 2007.

I walked through streets and avenues, I talked with university professors, civil servants of different levels and with workers from different non-governmental organizations (NGOs), as well as with 'anonymous' people. I also met and talked with members of various organizations. I visited several organizations dedicated to the most diverse purposes and structured in different ways.

It was essential to meet people who, together, fight for other ways of life based on attitudes based on values and principles that are more loving and life-oriented than those that seem to be the dominant ones today.

As stated initially, more than a synthesis in the form of a product, the value of this work lies in its procedural character. Therefore, I invite readers

---

31   ROLNIK, S. Cartografia sentimental: transformações contemporâneas do desejo. Porto Alegre: Sulina; Editora da UFRGS, 2006, p. 45-46.

32   ROLNIK, S. Cartografia ou de como pensar com o corpo vibrátil. Núcleo de Estudos e Pesquisas da Subjetividade da PUC/SP, 1987.

33   KASTRUP, V., op. cit.

34   ROLNIK, S., op. cit.

to go through the various stages of this work, marked by transformations, discoveries, emotions, constructions, deconstructions, and learnings, including from myself.

I hope that the work can affect readers in different ways, raising questions, doubts, questions, concerns, actions, and changes, especially towards more just, egalitarian, and solidary worlds.

It is important to emphasize that some texts are written with the present tenses, to preserve the moment of creation and insert the reader in the lived contexts. In some of the excerpts that I narrate I quote the names of those involved. In others, I choose not to name them. At other times, I replace the names of some of those involved with fictitious names, out of respect for privacy and considering that the most important thing, according to the purposes of this work, is to be able to share the experiences, the experiences, and what they can build, raise and teach.

I would also like to take this opportunity to point out that in the passages in which I bring and faithfully quote those who built this work with me, I put their statements in quotation marks and italics, with the sole intention of stressing that those are the voices of the participants in this process, even on the occasions when I do not quote them by name.

If nevertheless, somebody is offended at some point, I emphasize that this is not my intention and apologize in advance. I take this opportunity to stress, too, that all errors contained herein are my entire responsibility.

Evening on the Azorean coast
São Miguel island, Azores
May 17, 2009
Photo by Igor Vinicius Lima Valentim

III
SOLIDARITY ECONOMY: A BRIEF HISTORY

Solidarity Economy (SE) has origins that are difficult to demarcate, but the concept has been debated in Brazil and French-speaking literature, with this nomenclature, since the 1990s. In France, the concept was elaborated, above all, from the research developed in Crida (from the French *Centre de Recherche et d' Information sur la Démocratie et l'Autonomie*) under the coordination of Jean-Louis Laville, aiming to account for the proliferation of diverse socioeconomic initiatives[1].

In the European context, Solidarity Economy appears, according to João Roberto Lopes Pinto[2], as a counterpoint to the notion of Social Economy, affirming the necessary autonomy and political dimension of economic strategies for social insertion[3].

The introduction of the term Solidarity Economy in Brazil is attributed[4] to Paul Singer, initially in the article 'Solidarity Economy against Unemployment',

---

1   FRANÇA FILHO, G. C.; LAVILLE, J.-L. A Economia Solidária: uma abordagem internacional. Porto Alegre: Editora da UFRGS, 2004, p. 109.

2   PINTO, J. R. L. Economia Solidária: de volta à arte da associação. Porto Alegre: Editora da UFRGS, 2006, p. 30.

3   FRANÇA FILHO, G. C.; LAVILLE, J.-L., op. cit.

4   PINTO, J. R. L., op. cit., p. 27-28.

published in Folha de São Paulo newspaper, on July 11, 1996. Other similar concepts have also been elaborated, such as Socioeconomia Solidária[5],[6], Economia Popular Solidária[7] and Social Economy[8],[9], to name but a few.

In an article entitled "Towards a solidary economy - based on the Portuguese case", Rui Namorado[10] considers that the Solidarity Economy should be understood as an expression synonymous with Social Economy. However, Namorado's piece is exclusively theoretical, and do not investigate any concrete SE experience.

Bearing in mind that a detailed discussion about the contrasts between these different conceptual elaborations is not the focus of this book, I emphasize that even though they are focused on the reflection of a social phenomenon that is often similar, they all differ from each other.

By consulting the references cited here, readers who wish to delve into this conceptual discussion will find enough material to at least initiate such an undertaking. I focus on the concept of Solidarity Economy, considering that this is the one that has been most used to name the social phenomenon in question in recent decades.

Debates on SE have been expanding to several countries and aroused growing interest. In 2005, the first Portuguese congress dedicated to the theme of SE took place in the Autonomous Region of the Azores.

In October 2007, the Philippines hosted the first Asian SE Forum, and, in 2008, a seminar focused on Solidarity Economy was held in Coimbra, Portugal. In March 2009, the United States of America (USA) held its first forum dedicated to the same theme, after constituting in 2008 a network focused on the theme (USSEN or United States Solidarity Economy Network).

5   ARRUDA, M. Socioeconomia solidária: desenvolvimento de baixo para cima. Rio de Janeiro: Ed. PACS, 1998.

6   LISBOA, A. D. M. Economia Solidária e autogestão: imprecisões e limites. Revista de Administração de Empresas – RAE, v. 45, n. 3, p. 109-115, jul/sep 2005.

7   BERTUCCI, A. A.; SILVA, R. M. A. Vinte anos de economia popular solidária: trajetória da Cáritas Brasileira dos PACs à EPS. Brasília: Cáritas Brasileira, 2003.

8   FERREIRA, J. M. C. O papel do cooperativismo no desenvolvimento da economia social em Portugal. Verve, n. 2, p. 88-122, oct 2002.

9   NAMORADO, R. A Economia Social - Uma constelação de esperanças. Oficina do CES, n. 213, 2004. Available at: http://www.ces.uc.pt/publicacoes/oficina/213/213.pdf. Acessed on 27 aug 2005.

10   NAMORADO, R. Para uma economia solidária - a partir do caso português. Revista Crítica de Ciências Sociais, n. 84, 2009, p. 65-80.

SE concept has different conceptions in these different geographic regions and often within the same country. USA version[11] considers that it is an alternative framework of references aimed at economic development that is anchored in the principles of solidarity, equality in all dimensions, participatory democracy , sustainability, and pluralism. Also, according to the USSEN network, SE is in the process of construction, rejects one-size-fits-all solutions, and seeks transformation[12].

To Paul Singer, while discussing Brazilian contexts, SE historically emerged as a reaction against the injustices perpetrated by those who drive the development capitalist, a development that is not for everyone. Still according to him, "SE does not intend to oppose development, which, even being capitalist, makes humanity progress"[13].

People's need to find their own ways of creating work and income as a means of survival - together with unemployment - makes the Solidarity Economy appear as the solution for a huge number of people who no longer find space in the capitalist economy[14].

Although I would not say that this is a new phenomenon, it is noticeable, especially in the last two decades, the increasing number of people who, before fighting for survival alone or almost exclusively on their own, progressively organize themselves collectively under the nomenclature of the Solidarity Economy, including some associations and cooperatives.

It is important to note that SE concept was created by academics and is recognized mostly among professionals from academia, organizations considered to belong to the Third Sector (such as non-governmental organizations - NGOs), and within public management and policy makers.

The National Secretariat for Solidarity Economy was created in 2003 by the Brazilian State, within the Ministry of Labor and Employment (SENAES/MTE), responsible for public policies related to this other economy at the federal level. According to this governmental body, based on data present

---

11   USSEN. The U.S. Solidarity Economy Network (SEN), 13 nov 2008.

12   Idem.

13   SINGER, P. Desenvolvimento capitalista e desenvolvimento solidário. Estudos Avançados, v. 18, n. 51, p. 7-22, may/aug 2004, p. 11.

14   SINGER, P. A economia solidária vista a partir dos países do sul: Economia solidária no Brasil. In: Actas do Congresso internacional de economia solidária, Ponta Delgada. Centro de Estudos de Economia Solidária do Atlântico, p. 131-139, 2005, p. 133

in the latest version of the Atlas of Solidarity Economy and collected in a mapping throughout Brazil, more than 21,000 Solidarity Economy organizations are already accounted for[15].

One issue to be considered is that many of the organizations considered by different social actors - such as Universities, companies in the so-called Third Sector, and state institutions - to be part of SE do not consider themselves as such. In many cases, they do not even know the concept of 'Solidarity Economy'.

Some associations and cooperatives that today are considered to be part of SE precede any theoretical scheme. Besides, this concept is not always known and appropriated by the workers of these organizations, who, often on their initiative, organize themselves in forms of work that are before what, now, this 'new' concept seeks to name or project[16].

In this sense, while commenting on the experience of *Cooperativa de Novos Valores Ltd.* (Coopernova), some researchers[17] have already stated that the people who are part of it do not know and/or do not consider the concept of SE to be relevant. According to these authors, when asked about what they understand, where they apprehended and/or where they heard 'Solidarity Economy' for the first time, the people interviewed stated that they had not had any training on the subject.

In the sense of the above, there still seems to be a great distance between, on the one hand, the Solidarity Economy as a classification attributed by academics and/or by state entities and, on the other hand, the effective recognition as part of this movement by the members of the various associations and theoretically 'recognizable' cooperatives as belonging to SE.

It is important, then, to pay attention to the fact that SE is treated, understood, and operated in different ways, according to each social actor. It can be, simultaneously, understood as a public policy, social movement, the theme of economic/financial interest, academic concept, among other meanings. And even within each of these possibilities, SE still encompasses

---

15   SENAES. O que é Economia Solidária, 11 jul 2009. Ministério do Trabalho e Emprego, 2009.

16   KRAYCHETE, G. Economia popular solidária: sustentabilidade e transformação social. 2006, p. 11. Available at: http://www.capina.org.br. Acessed on 10 mar 2010.

17   BEIERSDORFF, M. B. et al. Educação e trabalho através da Economia Solidária. In: Anais do IV Encontro de Economia Solidária, São Paulo. EDUSP, 2006, p. 14-15.

diversities that are often irreconcilable.

Who belongs to the Solidarity Economy?

There is no consensus regarding which organizations can be considered as belonging to the Solidarity Economy since there is no uniform understanding about what the concept encompasses and labels.

In an effort to match the multiplicity of SE, I focus on those who earn their daily living by belonging to and working in organizations of this type. SE encompasses initiatives related, mostly, to collectively organized work and income generation. The examples range from associations of garbage collectors to cooperatives formed by workers who have taken control of failed or bankrupt industries.

These initiatives are built for different reasons and have a plurality of organizational configurations, management modes, and ways of dealing with the most diverse uncertainties and unforeseen circumstances, typical of life. They have varying degrees of institutionalization and, in most of them, there is an extreme preponderance of orality in interpersonal and collective relationships[18].

A distinctive feature of organizations considered to be part of the SE is that they are based on[19] values such as solidarity, self-management, participation, and egalitarianism, different from those underlying the capitalist logic.

The Solidarity Economy can be understood as a way of organizing economic activities in contrast to the prevailing capitalist form[20], since it theoretically has democratic economic management and, consequently, also of equality among all participants. In other words, everyone who works on them is also, at least in theory, an owner of the enterprise.

If the literature on SE considers that these organizations' members collectively fight for more humane ways of working, relating, and living, based on different principles than those associated to the capitalist logic,

---

18   VALENTIM, I. V. L. Economia Popular e Solidária no Brasil: uma questão de confiança interpessoal. In: XXIX Encontro da Associação Nacional de Pós-graduação e Pesquisa em Administração, Brasília. ANPAD, 2005.

19   SINGER, P. A recente ressurreição da economia solidária no Brasil. In: SANTOS, B. D. S. (Ed.). Produzir para viver: os caminhos da produção não capitalista. Lisboa: Edições Afrontamento, 2003. p. 71-107.

20   SINGER, P. A economia solidária vista a partir dos países do sul: Economia solidária no Brasil. In: Actas do Congresso internacional de economia solidária, Ponta Delgada. Centro de Estudos de Economia Solidária do Atlântico, 2005. p. 131-139, p. 138.

it is essential to emphasize that these values should not be understood as fixed or perennials.

I agree with Gabriel Kraychete when he claims[21] that it is not a matter of idealizing SE enterprises as if they were governed by values and practices based exclusively on solidarity relations, which would constitute the determining motivation of its members for the organization and daily management of these enterprises.

Daily life in societies in which capitalist logic is dominant presents numerous difficulties for the operationalization of values such as those mentioned in the previous paragraphs. These values can be better understood as objectives, targets we aim in the middle of daily struggles. So, like Selda Engelman[22], I try not to understand SE as a model, but as projects of organizations that are built and lived according to values such as cooperation and solidarity. In search of values like these.

In other words, in the concrete and continuous clash with expressions of capitalist logic, the Solidarity Economy would then encompass initiatives that they can seek, have as their 'north', and in many instances develop valuessuch as solidarity, egalitarianism and self-management, in continuous tension with those underlying the capitalist logic.

Therefore, it is important to emphasize that **Solidarity Economy can be understood as a concept-movement that concerns collective initiatives that seek, in continuous tension, values such as solidarity, egalitarianism, and self-management, different from those of capitalists, even though expressions and meanings of these values are diverse in their multiple manifestations.**

The desire to pursue these values seems to be more fundamental to the understanding of SE than the judgment of its supposed visible effectiveness. It may be richer not to look exclusively at what is done, but mainly at how it is done. In the words of Cleide Leitão,

> the difference then is in the walk, in the steps taken that gradually open other shortcuts, other paths for travelers who venture to walk through them. Thus, the fundamental difference is in the reading that we make of these contributions, in the meanings that we attribute to them and in the use that we make of them. [...] There are so many possible ways of looking, perceiving, feeling what multiple, differentiated, plural and singular practices weave and retain through the guile and tactics of

21   KRAYCHETE, G., op. cit., p. 14.

22   ENGELMAN, S. Trabalho e loucura: uma biopolítica dos afetos. Porto Alegre: Sulina; Editora da UFRGS, 2006, p. 10.

> those who practice them creating other appropriations and uses for what, in a first glance, you may want to be a totalizer[23].

There is no consensus on the understanding and treatment of SE as representative of initiatives that go against capitalist logic. Santos and Rodriguez[24] consider that it is a question of undertaking reforms and initiatives that arise within the capitalist system in which we live, but that facilitates and gives credibility to forms of economic organization and non-capitalist sociability.

Eugênia Motta brings a contribution based on lived research[25] in the Solidarity Economy: what this other economy brings as original is precisely a particular way of organizing elements that already exist, such as the experiences of popular education, the action of the Catholic Church in communities, self-managed job proposals, cooperativism, among others.

France Filho and Laville[26] postulate that SE cannot be considered a new economic form, but that it represents an unprecedented attempt to articulate with the 'traditional' capitalist economy. For them, these organizations do not fully fall within the scope of a capitalist organization, but neither do they represent a real break with this paradigm. According to these two authors, innovation in solidarity services is supported by reciprocity, "which leads the process of interactions through which services are developed"[27].

Paul Singer[28] is categorical when he says that the Solidarity Economy "is a creation in a continuous process led by workers fighting against capitalism". SE would be a social form of production that is historically

---

23   LEITÃO, C. F. Cartografia de imagens de práticas solidárias. In: Anais do VIII Congresso Luso-Afro-Brasileiro de Ciências Sociais, Coimbra. Centro de Estudos Sociais, 2004, p. 5-6.

24   SANTOS, B. D. S.; RODRÍGUEZ, C. Introdução: para ampliar o cânone da produção. In: SANTOS, B. D. S. (Ed.). Produzir para viver: os caminhos da produção não capitalista. Lisboa: Edições Afrontamento, 2003. p. 21-66, p. 26-27.

25   MOTTA, E. D. S. M. A "Outra Economia": um olhar etnográfico sobre a Economia Solidária. (2004). Dissertação de Mestrado (Mestrado em Antropologia Social) - Museu Nacional / PPGAS, Universidade Federal do Rio de Janeiro, Rio de Janeiro, 2004, p. 64.

26   FRANÇA FILHO, G. C.; LAVILLE, J.-L., op. cit.

27   FRANÇA FILHO, G. C.; LAVILLE, J.-L., op. cit., p. 105.

28   SINGER, P. Economia socialista. In: SINGER, P.; MACHADO, J. (Ed.). Economia socialista: socialismo em discussão. São Paulo: Fundação Perseu Abramo, 2000. p. 11-50, p. 13.

developed by contesting the capitalist organization of work[29]. The purpose of this other economy would be to make development more just, sharing its benefits and losses more evenly and less casually.

However, I disagree with Singer that this may be 'the cause' of the 'Solidarity Economy movement'. Within the scope of this work, I consider that during a movement, our thinking and our actions do not necessarily start in opposition but emerge in a set of forces among which there are oppositions. In other words, one movement does not necessarily arise from a criticism of another. Experiences, including those considered as SE, are points of creation of meaning[30] and not a reflection of a reality that is elsewhere, like a kind of capitalism that would be external to all of us.

The capitalist logic encourages suffering and deprivation for many people. However, to suppose that the construction of a movement like SE occurs in opposition to this logic as 'its cause' would be synonymous of disrespecting the multiplicity of meanings constructed by the people who are part of this other economy.

Many of the Solidarity Economy organizations, when looking for values and principles more focused on life than those that guide the current dominant logic, can represent viable and real alternatives to it. This does not imply that they do not encounter significant difficulties since they are always inserted and must compete with companies, values, behaviors, and capitalist stimuli.

SE initiatives bring together not only different types of activities, but people with different backgrounds, thoughts, ideological perspectives, and motivations. These organizations reflect the life stories not only of their founders but also of their members. The styles, personalities, values, and ways of being, especially of their leaders, have a significant impact on their routine and functioning[31].

Even though it is a difficult and complex task for an organization to act contrary to the capitalist economic paradigm, it is also not necessary to

---

29   SINGER, P. A economia solidária vista a partir dos países do sul: Economia solidária no Brasil. In: Actas do Congresso internacional de economia solidária, Ponta Delgada. Centro de Estudos de Economia Solidária do Atlântico, 2005. p. 131-139.

30   ROCHA, M. L. D.; AGUIAR, K. Pesquisa-intervenção e a produção de novas análises. Revista Psicologia Ciência e Profissão, n. 4, p. 64-73, 2003, p. 67.

31   VALENTIM, I. V. L., op. cit.

surrender to it[32]. The issue of social struggle must be valued, mainly because it proposes alternatives to change the situation. Santos and Rodríguez[33] follow this line and consider that insisting on the viability of alternatives does not imply an acceptance of what exists.

It is important to postulate that SE encompasses, as stated above, a plurality of forms. Perhaps a fundamental step is to be permanently careful not to fall into the trap of evaluating SE initiatives based on comparison and competition with the success indicators that guide capitalist logic. So, I strongly disagree that

> then, the disadvantage of the solidary company is due to its technological gap and its technical-professional lack of preparation, in terms of the skills already acquired and in the capacity for innovation. Accustomed to manual labor, poorly qualified, and imbued with a "firm culture", an employee who follows prescriptions, new entrepreneurs now need to deal with the unknown world of day-to-day administration and long-term management[34].

Comparing Solidarity Economy organizations with traditional capitalist enterprises or evaluating the former according to the assumptions of the latter would do nothing but demean them or try to further embrace them within this inhuman logic. Another example in this line is brought by the same author when he states that

> despite the weak bargaining power of the absolute majority of Solidarity Economy companies, even in those tied to outsourcing situations, the effort goes towards [...] easing the dependency situation, to achieve a better competitive position, inside the productive chain and before the final buyer[35].

Could it be that because we live in a dominant logic based on competition, the only solution left for us is to try to dive into this competition in search of victory and success? What risks do understandings like these bring to organizations that may present other values and other logic? It is very worrying to consider that SE is a 'poor's economy':

> looking at the nature of the projects of solidarity economy, the key finding is the fact that they provide, in some cases, the existence of

32   CASTEL, R. As metamorfoses da questão social. Petrópolis: Vozes, 1998.

33   SANTOS, B. D. S.; RODRÍGUEZ, C., op. cit., p. 23.

34   GAIGER, L. I. A economia solidária no Brasil e o sentido das novas formas de produção não capitalistas. CAYAPA - Revista Venezolana de Economía Social, n. 8, p. 9-37, dec 2004, p. 26, my highlight.

35   GAIGER, L. I., op. cit., p. 21, my highlight

> relations antagonistic social capitalism and, in many cases, preserve and revitalize social relationships, not capitalists, fundamental for the lives of the poor and for the individuals who live off their work[36].

I believe that from the moment we allow ourselves to dream with the intensities we experience in the various encounters we have, we open up and produce corresponding objects and modes of subjectification: this is what allows us to live the encounters, make them real[37].

I do not understand SE as radically as Singer when he says that this other economy consists of companies that effectively practice self-management without, however, being confused with cooperatives that employ wage earners[38]. Several of the more than twenty-one thousand Solidarity Economy enterprises documented in the latest Brazilian mapping of Solidarity Economy organizations[39] employs, on varying scales, salaried workers. However, can this fact be enough to mischaracterize a certain organization as belonging to the SE movement? I do not think so!

In day-to-day struggles for survival in a world dominated by capitalist logic, some of the organizations that have few employees, especially when this occurs temporarily, can actively seek supportive and life-oriented values.

It seems reasonable not to talk about Solidarity Economy when dealing with the so-called 'fakecoops'[40], that is, cooperatives created to take advantage of the legal characteristics of this legal form, but which base all their activities on salaried work, carried out at the service of managers who work as owners.

Even with difficulties, the SE encompasses examples that go, to a certain extent, in the opposite direction of what Maurizio Lazzarato[41] claims about unemployment as a mechanism for destroying cooperation between brains. If for many people cooperation becomes more difficult in the competitive and savage contemporary world, this other economy shows examples of

---

36   GAIGER, L. I., op. cit., p. 27, my highlight.

37   ROLNIK, S. Cartografia sentimental: transformações contemporâneas do desejo. Porto Alegre: Sulina; Editora da UFRGS, 2006, p. 45-46.

38   SINGER, P. A recente ressurreição da economia solidária no Brasil. In: SANTOS, B. D. S. (Ed.). Produzir para viver: os caminhos da produção não capitalista. Lisboa: Edições Afrontamento, 2003. p. 71-107, p. 73-74.

39   SENAES, op. cit.

40   SINGER, P., op. cit.

41   LAZZARATO, M. As revoluções do capitalismo. Rio de Janeiro: Civilização Brasileira, 2006.

organizations that originated precisely from situations of unemployment and difficulties in survival.

For a huge contingent, misery and unemployment have served precisely as factors of collective mobilization and can increase the creation of different alternatives:

> it is perceived that it is not simple to enhance the invention of other ways of working in the hegemonic capitalist context, where the need for survival is imperative. Such a need sometimes triggers creative potential. However, it is impossible not to understand these potentialities as the effects of poverty and social inequalities and it is in this sense that thinking about resistance strategies linked to the invention of other ways of working, does not mean a romantic and literary view of poverty and misery. It means adhering to the quest for the production of dignity and the recognition of the ability of men and women to reflect and produce their ways of living, working, and existing[42].

Therefore, when I speak of ES, I am not only referring to people who seek to work and generate income through cooperativism. There are possibilities for the emergence, based on relationships mediated by associated work, of new shared meanings, and new solidarities, which can requalify the meanings of work[43], production, consumption, exchanges, and, also, ways of thinking, feeling and living.

Solidarity Economy: Portuguese Conceptual Perspectives

Specifically in Portugal, the first publication on the Solidarity Economy concept dates to 2005 and was written by Rogério Roque Amaro[44], a university professor in Lisbon. Even though Roque Amaro's text is from 2005, according to him, the Solidarity Economy was born about 35 years ago.

In a theoretical perspective different from the others presented here in the previous section, the first publication about a Portuguese Solidarity Economy[45] considers that the SE concept would be established through common projects in a region known as Macaronesia, which involves the

---

42   TITTONI, J. Subjetivação e trabalho: reflexões sobre a Economia Solidária. In: VIII Congresso Luso-Afro Brasileiro de Ciências Sociais, sep 2004, Coimbra. Centro de Estudos Sociais, 2004, p. 9-10.

43   PINTO, J. R. L., op. cit., p. 16.

44   AMARO, R. R. Reflexões sobre a economia solidária. In: Actas do Congresso internacional de economia solidária, 29-30 sep 2005, Ponta Delgada. Centro de estudos de economia solidária do atlântico, 2005. p. 17-29.

45   Idem.

Azores, Cape Verde, the Canaries, and Madeira. However, the publication does not mention what these common projects would be.

Macaronesian Solidarity Economy is treated as a tool in the fight against poverty and social exclusion, given the worsening social inequalities and the new situations of poverty[46]. This understanding is corroborated by Cunha when he affirms that one of the objectives of SE would be to increase the employability of people who are in poverty and/or in social exclusion"[47].

Macaronesian SE would be "the most comprehensive, demanding, and broad of all, since it asserts itself as a Multidimensional, Integrated and Life-Encountering Economy in all its aspects"[48]. However, the search for "integrated competitiveness of these organizations, seeking to reconcile it with their democratic management - whenever possible"[49] is among the principles related to this version of the SE.

It seems at least conflicting a search for competitiveness reconciled only when possible with democratic management.

A reference to a specific organization belonging to SE in Portugal is brought by Cunha when he comments on the creation, in the Azores, of the Regional Cooperative of Solidarity Economy of the Azores (Cresaçor), which "has been allowing the study and construction of a system of continuous sustainability of the Solidarity Economy Movement"[50].

The article entitled "The economy is either supportive or fratricidal"[51], by José Portela, proposes to think about SE "from the ground up" and reflects on two non-governmental organizations of public benefit whose activities intertwine with four micro-entrepreneurs and their productive units. The author investigates these NGOs that support microentrepreneurs, as well as the solidarities and economies present in the productive units of the latter. It is interesting to note that, for Portela[52], within the scope of what he debates in

---

46   AMARO, R. R., op. cit., p. 29.

47   CUNHA, D. Intervenção do secretário regional dos assuntos sociais do governo regional dos Açores. In: Actas do Congresso internacional de Economia Solidária, 29-30 sep 2005, Ponta Delgada. Centro de estudos de economia solidária do atlântico, 2005. p. 13-15, p. 13.

48   AMARO, R. R., op. cit., p. 20.

49   AMARO, R. R., op. cit., p. 21.

50   CUNHA, D., op. cit., p. 15.

51   PORTELA, J. A economia ou é solidária ou é fratricida. Revista Crítica de Ciências Sociais, n. 84, p. 115-152, 2009, p. 115.

52   Idem.

this article, microentrepreneurs can be considered as representatives of SE in Portugal. This conception goes in the opposite direction to that of a more collective nature, adopted in this work, which considers that associations and cooperatives - that is, collective organizations - would belong to this other economy.

Even though Portela[53] investigates what he considers as "ground" examples of SE in Portugal, the micro-entrepreneurship that he addresses in his research does not include Portuguese associations or cooperatives and has a very different conception from that of SE adopted here.

I seek to investigate associations and cooperatives in Portugal that fight for values such as egalitarianism, solidarity, self-management, and the primacy of the human over the capital.

The theories about SE in Portugal mentioned above seem even irreconcilable, in some respects, with some of Brazilian versions on the same concept. However, as seen in the previous paragraphs, it was not possible to find details about in-depth research carried out in organizations belonging to this other economy, nor an estimate of how many exist, what type of work they do, or how the experiences and relationships within from them.

It seems necessary, then, to dive into the universe of this other economy, to live these experiences, so that one can better deal with the phenomena labeled by the concept 'Solidarity Economy' in its potentialities.

---

53   Idem.

Openness
São Miguel island, Azores
May 16, 2009
Photo by Igor Vinicius Lima Valentim

IV
SOLIDARITY ECONOMY
IN PORTUGAL

For some years now, as I have previously mentioned, Solidarity Economy - and not only Social Economy - has also been discussed[1,2,3,4] in Portugal, although the latter concept[5,6] is present in the Constitution of the Portuguese Republic.

Living in Lisbon since October 2007, and from my experiences with

---

1   AMARO, R. R. Reflexões sobre a economia solidária. In. Actas do Congresso internacional de economia solidária, 29-30 sep 2005, Ponta Delgada. Centro de estudos de economia solidária do atlântico, 2005. p. 17-29.

2   AMARO, R. R.; MADELINO, F. Economia Solidária. Contributos para um conceito. 2. ed. Ponta Delgada: Projecto CORES, 2006.

3   CUNHA, D. Intervenção do secretário regional dos assuntos sociais do governo regional dos Açores. In: Actas do Congresso internacional de Economia Solidária, 29-30 sep 2005, Ponta Delgada. Centro de estudos de economia solidária do atlântico, 2005. p. 13-15.

4   PORTELA, J. A economia ou é solidária ou é fratricida. Revista Crítica de Ciências Sociais, n. 84, p. 115-152, 2009.

5   GOVERNO DOS AÇORES. Empresas e Economia Solidária dão emprego a 210 pessoas nos Açores. Portal do Governo dos Açores. Ponta Delgada, 29 de Setembro de 2005. Available at: http://edt gra.azores.gov.pt/Portal. Accessed on: 18 oct 2008.

6   GOVERNO DOS AÇORES. Intervenção do presidente do Governo na abertura de uma mesa redonda sobre Pobreza e Exclusão. Portal do Governo dos Açores. Ponta Delgada, 16 de Outubro de 2007. Available at: http://edtgra.azores.gov.pt/Portal. Accessed on: 18 oct 2008.

associations of scavengers (recyclable materials street collectors) in Brazil[7], I started to notice that, in large Portuguese cities, there were huge amounts of recyclable solid waste on the streets. While in Portugal I had never noticed any scavenger on the streets, in Brazil several people survived precisely from the collection and sale of these materials.

I tried to seek, firstly, associations, and cooperatives of scavengers in Portugal. Would they also exist in the Iberian country, as well as in Brazil, Argentina, Colombia, India, and Egypt? A research is partly published in a book chapter[8].

I also participated in a seminar dedicated to discussing solid waste and recycling policies in Europe. It was held in Óbidos, Portugal, during 2008. On the occasion, I had the chance to speak with representatives of several organizations related to the sector, such as the Portuguese Association for the Environment (APA) and Ponto Verde Society (SPV).

It was possible to understand that, in Portugal, anyone needs to have, to carry out commercial transactions with the waste described above, an organization legally institutionalized and certified by SPV, the entity responsible for policies related to waste treatment and recycling in Portugal, composed of several public and private actors.

It would not be an exaggeration to say that SPV is one of the most important organizations when it comes to garbage and/or recycling in Portugal. It carries out media campaigns encouraging recycling, and it determines through its policies which types of materials are considered recyclable and which should be sent directly to landfills.

I was able to understand that the waste must be collected only and exclusively by companies certified by SPV, that is, its partners, which may or may not be city councils. It is worth remembering that SPV receives fees from all those organizations whose activities produce waste.

After being collected, solid waste is sent to be treated by recycling companies also accredited by SPV according to each geographic region.

If a person or group decides to collect cardboard boxes on the streets to recycle and/or sell them, they are doing something illegal and subject to

---

7   CARRION, R. S. M.; VALENTIM, I. V. L.; HELLWIG, B. C. Residência Solidária UFRGS: vivência de universitários com o desenvolvimento de uma tecnologia social. Porto Alegre: Editora da UFRGS, 2006.

8   VALENTIM, I. V. L. Are we fighting a single enemy? Looking for alternatives to capitalism with garbage workers. In: TITTENBRUN, J. (Ed.). Capitalism or Capitalisms? Szczecin: MyBook, 2009, p. 183-201.

sanctions.

Due to all these restrictions, mainly related to economic interests, I did not find scavengers working on their own on the streets in Portugal, much less any association or cooperative.

Not having found associations of workers dedicated to the theme of garbage in mainland Portugal[9], I began to search, in academic publications on the theme of Solidarity Economy, for examples of organizations on Portuguese soil dedicated to the theme.

I was surprised, first, by the small number of academic texts dedicated to SE as it happens in Portugal. It was very difficult to find concrete SE examples, even in the few academic publications on the subject already mentioned in the last section of the previous chapter. In other words, these publications seem more dedicated to theorizing about a Portuguese version of Solidarity Economy, instead of carrying out in-depth investigations with members of associations and cooperatives in Portugal. In addition to these issues, the publications indicated a greater presence of Portuguese SE organizations in island territories (Azores and, to a lesser extent, Madeira).

During research carried out in libraries, databases, academic journals, as well as in search engines on the internet, such as Google and Google academic, I showed the scarce amount of publications related to SE in the Azorean archipelago. The few found[10] show a descriptive/ informative character about events related to the theme, but I was unable to locate in-depth academic investigations on the Solidarity Economy phenomenon in the locality.

According to the Azorean regional government, SE generates hundreds of jobs in the Azores archipelago[11] and is the target of specific public policies[12]. However, one of the Azorean public policies guidelines for the SE mentions the creation of insertion companies, incubated essentially

---

9   Idem.

10   AMARO, R. R., op. cit.; CUNHA, D., op. cit.; AMARO, R. R.; MADELINO, F., op. cit.

11   GOVERNO DOS AÇORES. Empresas e Economia Solidária dão emprego a 210 pessoas nos Açores. Portal do Governo dos Açores. Ponta Delgada, 29 de Setembro de 2005. Available at: http://cdt-gia.azores.gov.pt/Portal. Accessed on: 18 oct 2008.

12   GOVERNO DOS AÇORES. Intervenção do presidente do Governo na abertura de uma mesa redonda sobre Pobreza e Exclusão. Portal do Governo dos Açores. Ponta Delgada, 16 de Outubro de 2007. Available at: http://edtgra.azores. gov.pt/Portal. Accessed on: 18 oct 2008.

by private institutions of social solidarity (IPSS), aimed mainly at the integration of people in serious situations of exclusion[13]. Would Solidarity Economy organizations be treated as a temporary space for the insertion of people, later to be hired by heterogeneous 'traditional' enterprises?

With little information on the topic and looking for clues about experiences related to SE, I undertook a documentary research[14] to understand how the Solidarity Economy was portrayed by the Azorean media. I investigated media representations of SE in *Diário dos Açores* newspaper, and analyzed journalistic articles related to the theme. The news selection process was carried out by searching the electronic archive of that newspaper using keywords and expressions that would provide indications about how the topic is treated.

In total, the research was carried out with thirteen keywords, since in addition to 'Solidarity Economy' were also included: associativism, self-management, fair trade, solidary consumption, cooperativism, labor economy, popular economy, social economy, Solidary socioeconomy, solidarity finance, social currency, and solidarity economic enterprises.

I could see that, in the news published in 2008 by the oldest Azorean newspaper, SE organizations are named as companies. Nevertheless, the pieces establish links between SE and entrepreneurship, as well as with a 'social market economy'. These relationships give valuable clues regarding the construction of meanings in the sphere of SE: towards the reproduction and assimilation of the values underlying the currently dominant capitalist logic.

Even more intriguing was the understanding that none of the articles had voices of members of organizations of Solidarity Economy, Social Economy, cooperatives and/or associations.

In other words, in the scope of the analysis developed, *Diário dos Açores* gave voice only to people considered 'experts' in their areas of activity: university professors, researchers, career politicians, responsible for projects, among others. I could not find the voice of workers directly involved in the public policies in question, such as the members of SE organizations.

If a reader wished to find only one organization that was portrayed as a SE example throughout 2008, one would end the year without the possibility of identifying it in the articles published by Diário dos Açores

---

13   CUNHA, D., op. cit, p. 13.

14   VALENTIM, I. V. L. Economia Solidária nos Açores: um retrato de suas representações e construções midiáticas no Diário dos Açores. Anais do XI Congresso Ibero-Americano de Comunicação, 16-19 abril 2009, Funchal, 2009.

newspaper. Furthermore, if one tried to understand what this other economy consists of, one probably would not find satisfactory answers either.

I tried to schedule meetings with Professor Ronaldo Rosa Amparo to get more clues about the concept of the Solidarity Economy in Portugal, between April 2008 and December 2009, but they were cancelled at three different times.

I also contacted the University of the Azores (UAC), looking for a professor dedicated to the subject of SE. Maurício Tinoco, a member of the Center for Social Studies, replied by email and we got to exchange more than ten messages. In one of these e-mails, the professor told me that there were no people dedicated to the subject of SE at UAC, but that I could obtain more information from the Institute for Social Action of the Azores Government, in the person of Carlos Bastos. He also said, in another message, that he had already worked with ES on São Miguel Island, but that *"the modern Solidary Economy in Portugal is a top initiative. That is a State initiative"*.

I was even more intrigued and sure that it made all the difference for me, due to my goals, to find publications dedicated to the investigation of some 'living example' of Solidarity Economy in the Azores. And not just that. It was urgent **to live** Solidarity Economy in Portugal.

José Maria Carvalho Ferreira (Zé Maria), my advisor during my Ph.D. in Sociology[15], told me he had no knowledge about organizations of this type in mainland Portugal, but signaled positively about the possibility of finding them on São Miguel island (Azores largest island). With the impossibility of finding indications about living examples of SE in mainland Portugal, I decided that I would move to Azores, after conversations with Maurício Tinoco by email and with my advisor and friend Zé Maria.

Exactly one week before embarking to São Miguel island I managed, on the fourth try, to be received by Ronaldo Rosa Amparo in his office in Lisbon. We talked for about forty minutes and he explained to me that perhaps the biggest reason why I did not find publications about Portuguese SE organizations was that he was not dedicated to writing.

In the same conversation, he explained to me a little about what he

---

15   PhD in Economic and Organizational Sociology, carried out at SOCIUS - Research Center in Economic and Organizational Sociology, within the scope of the Higher Institute of Economics and Management (ISEG), of the University of Lisbon. The Ph.D. was completed on December 16, 2011 and the public jury is available, on video, at http://www.youtube.com/watch?v=1gx9916EH2w. The experiences narrated here are an integral part of those that contributed to the construction of the doctoral thesis.

understands about SE as it happens in Portugal, speaking specifically about the Azorean context. He told me about two examples of SE organizations, which I could visit on São Miguel island since I was already moving there: Azores Regional Solidarity Economy Cooperative (Cresaçor), dedicated to various activities and with 'different skills' and Celeiro da Terra, dedicated to food production.

Ronaldo mentioned that I should also look for Jaime Marins, director of the Institute for Social Action in the Autonomous Region, and one of the biggest players in the theme since its 'creation'. When Ronaldo spoke of 'creation', I immediately remembered the email exchanged with Maurício Tinoco. Would the Azorean SE really be a movement 'created' out of the state initiative – top-down – and not from the collective mobilization of people – bottom-up?

With the indications of Ronaldo, Maurício and Zé Maria, I moved to São Miguel Island, in the Autonomous Region of the Azores, in April 2009, without ever having been there. Below, I share many of the moments of this trajectory, narrating them in the present tense, thus preserving the form of elaboration of the diaries that I built and that help me, today, to share in the form of a book. I also emphasize that I preserve in italics the speeches of those who built these experiences with me.

Arriving at Ponta Delgada airport

I am landing at João Paulo II airport, São Miguel island, on April 26, 2009, around 9:30 am. After collecting the luggage, I look for the Solidarity Economy store at the airport. It is not difficult to find it, as there are few stores, and they are all located on the first floor.

The store's facade mentions the name Solidarity Economy in addition to adventure and tourism. In the exterior showcase, it is possible to see products of the most diverse types, such as hand-painted porcelain, liquors, cookies. I decide to go in and talk to the attendant who, very friendly, speaks to me slowly. The Azorean accent is very different from Lisbon's.

The store also offers adventure tourism and I start asking for explanations, mentioning that I was born in Rio de Janeiro, Brazil, and that my knowledge of SE is based on some Brazilian experiences. The attendant soon shows me some women's blouses made by cooperatives in Brazil and says that in São Miguel island the same thing happens, with associations performing the same work that exists in Brazil. She hands me a brochure and explains that the central office can give me more details about the adventure tourism, which she confesses she does not know.

I then ask if the airport store is open directly, and she says yes, from 7:30 am to 9:00 pm, every day, including Sundays and holidays. She comments that many products from SE member organizations are sold there, including several handmade ones. She is not part of any SE association and says she is just an employee: Andressa. According to her, store visitors do not know about Solidarity Economy, *"they are not very aware of it yet"*, and many arrive there and do not even look at the store's name. The lack of knowledge about the SE and the origin of the products appears as an interesting point.

Andressa continues and says that the store does not have only SE products, otherwise it would not survive. I show my surprise and she explains that those who come from outside the island can appreciate it, but that those who live there do not know and are not very interested. Tea is one of the items that sell the most, and non-SE products end up financially compensating others, balancing the store's accounts.

The competition with products from traditional private companies appears strongly and gives rise to reflections related to the store's context. A store of a SE cooperative (Cresaçor) , supposedly in the name of its financial sustainability also sells products that are in no way related to the values of this other economy.

Cookies, jams, liqueurs, and hand-painted articles are made by SE workers, but *"people don't value it"*. There have been cases where people have bought products because they are from SE, but this usually happens to people outside the Azores. Andressa reinforces that residents do not have this notion and *"live a lot on the surface"*, making mention of a life of appearances, superficial, values that are widespread in our societies.

I ask if the SE products that are sold there are more expensive than similar ones from organizations that are not considered as belonging to SE. Andressa tells me that *"it depends"*, before going around the store with me and pointing out the prices of some of the items sold. She explains that many SE products that are marketed there are also sold in supermarkets, that is, in the 'traditional' distribution market. Andressa says that at the Cresaçor store these products turn out to be cheaper, but she cannot say why, although she risks it because the markets put the price they want.

Andressa thinks that organizations need to penetrate the 'traditional' distribution network and have their products sold "everywhere": if they were sold in just one place, they would not be able to get conditions to survive: *"things are difficult and people they have to do it anyway"*, referring to the island's economic situation.

An interesting observation made by Andressa regarding the SE products sold there on the island of São Miguel is that they are not essential items, *"that you must buy"*, but things that you have to try. These are products that people *"go through the store and often don't even look at... not something you need, do you see?"*.

Another interesting point is that São Miguel island is not a shopping destination. Tourists buy only what they think they should, but do not visit the island thinking about shopping, which would have a direct impact on this issue of marketing of products. On the store's wall there is a glass board with the name of Cresaçor participant organizations, but Andressa explains that some of those are no longer part of the cooperative, while different others have already joined.

Leaving the store, I head to Laranjeiras University Residence, which belongs to the UAC and where I will reside for the next few months. There are no buses from the airport to the city center, according to my information. The taxi costs ten Euros, and the distance is short. There is no meter and the driver charges me verbally.

Around noon I go out to have lunch and walk around the city on foot. It takes me about forty-five minutes to Portas do Mar, a complex of bars, restaurants, and some 'designer' stores, right next to the Marina and part of Ponta Delgada Maritime Terminal area. On the way, I walk through practically empty streets and I think this is because it is a Sunday and a Sunday just after a national holiday, such as April 25 in Portugal.

It is interesting to note that close to Portas do Mar there is a public swimming pool built on the rocks, using seawater like a pool. There are restrooms and sunbeds in a cement area, at the cost of one Euro per day.

There are also imported perfume stores and snack bars, in addition to Azores store, which has some SE products, even though this is not written anywhere, and I only find out when circulating through the exhibited goods.

University of the Azores: Social Studies Center

Just two days after my arrival on the island, I have an appointment at 9.30 am with Maurício Tinoco, a UAC professor. He comments that he is from Lisbon and came to the Azores 16 or 17 years ago.

Maurício says he is one of the forerunners of the Social Economy in the Azores, *"without false modesty and without arrogance"*. In his speech, he alternates the terms 'Social Economy' and 'Solidarity Economy' as if they were synonymous, and says that a major motivator of the theme on the island was the fact that people (target of public policies for social inclusion), even after professional training, they had no way to fit into the job market, because nobody wanted them, and *"if you don't have a job, you invent yourself"*.

When asked about the reasons for choosing to research the Azorean archipelago, I explain a little about my trajectory and the motivations for wanting to live SE in the archipelago, as well as better understand what happens when talking about Solidarity Economy in the Azores. Maurício also says that if it were not for Liberato Fernandes, associativism and cooperativism would not have developed so much, they would not have gained so much expression in the Azores. Maurício comments on a series of spinouts, that is, several associations being created from existing associations.

During our email conversations, as already highlighted in this chapter, Maurício always emphasized that he considered SE in the Azores an "initiative from the top", that is, a phenomenon created by the State's initiative, and not from the collective mobilization of people.

Now, face to face, he says that SE in the Azores emerged as a movement from collective mobilization, and that the creation of state laws in this respect took place from what already existed in the field. Even more intriguing is to hear Maurício say that he was, to a great extent, the precursor of SE in the Azores when he worked at the Institute for Social Action (IAS), in which Jaime Marins would be his 'right hand'.

I am intrigued: how can SE in the Azores be an *"initiative from above"*, initiated by the government and at the same time have emerged from collective mobilization?

Maurício says that when he worked at IAS, *"more or less 16 years ago"*, there was only one cooperative on São Miguel island, of which he does not remember the name. This cooperative was in Lagoa and was created from the collective mobilization of women articulated by a social worker who later was elected deputy, Letícia Moura. The cooperative would be made up of deaf women who made cookies and cakes as a way of survival.

Maurício comments that he does not remember the name of this organization, but that it was the first cooperative on the island, having appeared before his work at IAS, a period in which, together with Jaime Marins, 'created' several cooperatives.

He comments on the example of Kairós, a cooperative that emerged as an incubator for Solidarity Economy initiatives and of which he was one of the founders, along with eleven other people, among whom none were workers. An initiative *"from above"*, therefore. This information reinforces what Maurício had stated by email, about SE being treated as a representative of initiatives created from above. At the same time, it points to the fact that there may be other associations and cooperatives, arising from collective mobilization, which may not be recognized by the government as SE representatives, but that are supported by values of this other economy. How to find this cooperative of an unknown name?

Finally, he asks what I will do for lunch and comments that we can have lunch together to talk about other issues. He says that he expects two things from me, *"being very sincere"*: to expand his network of contacts in a research topic in which he is not very active today, and to participate in my Ph.D. jury, considering that this would count a lot for his assessment at UAC: *"I am not a full professor yet, but I want to be"*.

University of the Azores: Entrepreneurship Center

On May 5, 2009, I go to the Center to talk to Carlos Faias, a supposed connoisseur of the Azorean SE. However, upon arriving, I am informed that it is no longer working there: *"You should talk to Valter Souza"*, current coordinator, for more information. Valter asks me what took me there and what I want to know. I explain first what I am doing and say that when talking about SE in Portugal, Azores is always mentioned: *"Carlos Faias would be a suitable person because he worked at Cresaçor"*.

Once again, I notice that everything that is said about SE in the Azores seems to be linked to Cresaçor, the person of Rosa Amparo and IAS, all interconnected.

I ask if today there is any relationship between the UAC Entrepreneurship Center and SE, and he says that their performance is much more focused on micro-entrepreneurs who want to start new companies. There is even a microcredit protocol with the private bank Millenium BCP: nothing related to SE, since it is only hoped that people will be able to find or create jobs on their own.

UAC has an Entrepreneurship course, taught in Economics and Management programs, and offered to Social Work undergraduate students. I ask if there is any relationship with SE in this chair and his answer brings interesting information to reflect: *"the only part [that has to do with SE] is the chapter that we put on Social Responsibility"*. In his view, then, Solidarity Economy is linked to Social Responsibility.

Valter Souza arrives and enters the room. He says he knows Rosa Amparo and asks if I am going to be at the Solidarity Economy Congress in two days, which I answer positively. Valter asks me if I know Amélia, from Cresaçor, and Janaína Lordes, from the Association of the Center for Studies in Solidarity Economy of the Azores (ACEESA).

I reply that I know Janaína since she and Rosa Amparo invited me to participate in that congress. Valter says: *"Amélia Siqueira is in charge of Cresaçor, which is the organization we have here in the Azores that works the most with SE, together with the policies developed by the Regional Government"*.

It is through Cresaçor that certain people, who have been unemployed for a long time, are inserted in the labor market, which makes me feel that Solidarity Economy may be understood as something temporary for the Azorean Government: *"Cresaçor is a cooperative of social solidarity, extremely operated by the Regional Government. The government makes the policy and Cresaçor executes it. Amélia is a very nice person"*.

Valter comments that, in his view, SE is extremely recent in the Azores, which seems to be somewhat contradictory to Rosa Amparo's view that the concept has existed in the archipelago since the mid-1990s. He considers that the problems faced in Brazil do not exist here and he speaks of microcredit and entrepreneurship as possibilities for reducing unemployment, considering that *"that we increasingly have to create our own jobs"*.

I am grateful for receiving me with open doors and Valter says that he will always be available if I need more information. Besides, he comments that if I need workspace/infrastructure while on the island, I can use the computer and internet at the UAC Entrepreneurship Center.

II Solidarity Economy Congress of the Azores

During the II Solidarity Economy Congress of the Azores, which took place on the 7th and 8th of May 2009 (the 1st edition took place in 2005), representatives of several organizations considered to belong to SE expose their experiences to the participants.

Academic professionals from different universities and localities, as well as members of the Azorean Regional Government also make presentations. Among the organizations present, I highlight Servelar, Cresaçor, and Celeiro da Terra cooperative.

Honorato Cordeiro, from Celeiro da Terra, calls himself secretary of the cooperative's management, in addition to a social service technician at a school. He arrives for the presentation of a suit, dressed as an executive of any multinational would be at a similar event.

Celeiro da Terra was created in 1998, under Valorizar project, as a social solidarity cooperative. This project was promoted by the Social and Parochial Center of Ribeira Quente (the cooperative is located in this village), since there was a *"need to implement the project Valuing Against Poverty"*, with the aim of *"integrating disadvantaged groups"*.

Today, the cooperative has 95 associates, but until 2007 it already had 190 'trainees' through IAS. It has a coordinator, five employees working in the kitchen, five in handicrafts, one at a kiosk in Vila da Povoação and one in a handicraft store in Furnas, in addition to another employee in the distribution and one in management.

The term used by Honorato to make a reference to Celeiro da Terra workers is noteworthy: *"employees"*. After all, who are hired employees and who are the associates? Who hires employees if they are not members? How is the co-op management? And what do the trainees do? What differences are there between trainees, associates, and employees?

During Honorato's presentation, he focuses a lot on production numbers, production capacity, shifts, consumed raw materials, among others. However, nothing about what the cooperative represents for the ones who work there.

I cannot understand the difference between the presentation of this cooperative and the presentation of any contemporary corporation, since what I see are slides that deal only with production, marketing, sales, among others, that is, management, analysis tools and presentation of an organization focused exclusively on profit.

Honorato mentions that Celeiro da Terra aims to *"increase jobs, employ more people"*, in addition to expanding its headquarters, production, and commercial network. They intend to move towards financial autonomy, without forgetting the solidarity component of the project.

Once again, the speech of the cooperative representative draws attention: *"without forgetting the solidarity component of the project"*, that is, solidarity is treated merely as a component of the project.

The following presentation is made by Ricardo Teixeira, from Servelar. He also arrives dressed in a suit and says that the organization was created on

Madeira Island in 2006, as an insertion company. Servelar is dedicated to gardening and cleaning services, but Ricardo does not mention how it was created, neither of whom was the initiative. Among the 'employee', everyone actively participates, and 'associates' get involved in the company's regular meetings. The company's objectives are to create jobs and to finance and sustain itself.

Ricardo also explains that the workers go through a training that lasts six months, in which contents related to cooperativism are not included. The employment contracts last for 24 months and employees have the possibility of receiving a performance bonus based on monthly assessments of their productivity and relationship with customers, colleagues, and managers.

Regarding the company's management, Ricardo says that there is a sociologist, hired as a service provider, a coordinator (also hired), and seven employees, with an average age of 35 to 40 years. The company's income was approximately 35 thousand euros in 2009, and Ricardo comments that some of the employees leave the company for the job market, but he does not explain why. When he talks about future investments to be made – all mainly financial – he does not mention any type of plan related to the people who are part of the organization.

Servelar has a partnership established with the Employment Institute of the Autonomous Region of Madeira (IP-RAM). The presentation ends with an institutional video that reminds those of large corporations. At the end of the video, are displayed:

a) an interview with an employee of the company of about 40 years of age who, in his speech, treats work as a responsibility and the good worker as one who arrives on time, is never absent and is very much disciplined.

b) an interview with a 37-year-old employee who says she is happy to work with a cell phone and that her life is 'five stars', very grateful.

c) an interview with the Mayor of São Vicente, who says: "*this company is a partner of the municipality to create jobs so that people can live with their work*".

Next, Amélia Siqueira presents the presentation of Cresaçor. She calls herself the organization's General Secretary and calls her presentation "*Cresaçor as a pillar of Solidarity Economy in the Azores*". This is very interesting, as it can provide clues as to how SE concept itself came to be used in the autonomous region.

Cresaçor emerged in 1999 as a cooperative of companies: initially two, Aurora Social and Kairos, in a fight against poverty and social exclusion. In

2000, it started to be considered a social solidarity cooperative, but Amélia does not comment on who created this *"umbrella cooperative"*.

Today, one of Cresaçor goals is to support the creation and sustainability of micro companies dedicated to social insertion. It has 26 employees in technical and administrative areas, four dedicated to catering, three to sales, and two interns in Tourism. Amélia considers that the team has a significant dimension and that it is growing. Cresaçor focuses on Social Responsibility indicators related to the efficiency and quality of its members (other SE organizations). It is important to note that Amélia refers to the quality of products sold by cooperatives participating in Cresaçor.

In the area of training, Cresaçor works in the development of skills for "social entrepreneurs", mixing entrepreneurship with the issue of social responsibility, and using this as an instrument for the insertion of people into the traditional labor market. One more presentation that links SE to temporary work, destined to (re)insert people into jobs in the 'traditional' labor market.

Today Cresaçor has twenty-one cooperatives, that is, twenty-one associations and cooperatives, which Amélia makes a point of naming one by one. Some principles of action of the organization are:

a) maximization of the concept of cooperation;

b) reinforcement of intervention strategies to improve the quality of products and conquer more market;

c) potentization of projects and applications for support from Portuguese government funding and at the level of the European community;

d) social marketing, strengthening the Solidarity Economy movement in the Azores, within which the CORES brand - present in the Azores, Canaries, and Madeira - created a SE certification seal, that is, a seal that attests a certain organization 'belongs to Solidarity Economy';

e) investigation/action processes. Amélia shows a photo of the first class of the master's in social and Solidarity Economy, coordinated by Rosa Amparo, of which she was a member.

Cresaçor seems to act based on a framework that was built in advance, and not to seek a joint construction of action plans with organizations in the field. It is also possible to see that profit is treated as a guiding criterion for insertion companies. In what is seen as key factors for the success of these companies, I see nothing related to what they represent to people. People seem to be treated as employees of any corporation. Amélia gives an example of success within SE: a man who created a bar in December 2007 and, even with difficulties in management and accounting, could create his job *"through his effort and persistence"*.

After the presentation, Ronaldo Rosa Amparo talks about the tensions that are present in the relationships between Solidarity Economy, private companies, and the State. Cresaçor is one of the organizations involved in microfinance in the Azores. He considers that Solidarity Economy works in various directions, among which microcredit is an important tool in the fight against poverty, although the concept of entrepreneurship is not necessarily linked to SE in his view.

It is incredible to notice how SE is seen as an economy of the poor, and not something related to an autonomous movement of people, as a collective initiative and/or social movement.

The event also hosts a presentation by the Mayor of Ponta Delgada, the island biggest city. During his speech, he addresses issues related to social inclusion, alternative models, and the need to develop new forms of entrepreneurship. He says that training, knowledge, and creativity are the basis for the self-sustainability of the SE organizations and that we need to apply *"efficiency and good management"* to this other economy.

In the end, it is possible to notice that he does not mention, at any time, the initiatives that already exist which were created bottom-up, from ground movement, always focusing, and again, like the other speakers, on the initiatives created for people, from the state or other organizations, but not organizations that emerged from popular collective mobilization.

On the second day of the congress, I deliver my presentation and some of the participants go to lunch together. I ask Ronaldo what he thought of the congress, and he says that he did not like the afternoon of the previous day, because he knows all the organizations and that they are not developed the way they were presented: *"in a totally mercantile way, as if they were normal capitalist companies, since from the presentations it seemed that they had nothing of Solidarity Economy"*.

I ask Jean-Louis Laville the same question, who replies that, from what he saw the previous day, he thought a lot about isomorphism, about how these organizations use the same discourse as capitalist companies. He returns the question to me and I say that I was surprised by the fact that the management of all organizations seems totally separate from their activities. He comments that in France self-management in SE organizations does not always occur, but that, even when management is carried out by a 'separate' person, in cases where members of the organizations do not want to *"get into it"*, members interfere in the decisions and directions of organizations.

Institute for Social Action

After indications by Ronaldo Rosa Amparo and Maurício Tinoco, I visit the Institute for Social Action (IAS) headquarters to talk to Jaime Marins, its director. The room is on the building's top floor, whose architecture brings undeniable hierarchical elements[16]. Upon being invited in, I discover that the meeting will also include Mariléia, a sociologist responsible for the 'mapping' of SE promoted by IAS, and Carlos Bastos, head of an IAS division.

I speak of my desire to understand why the concept of Solidarity Economy is currently taking shape in Portugal, even though Social Economy is the one present in the Portuguese Constitution. I comment on the recommendations of Rosa Amparo and Maurício Tinoco (who said he had already worked with Jaime).

Carlos begins introduces himself as the Head of IAS Planning division. Next, Mariléia says that she is on the IAS team responsible for SE and socio-institutional development, created not long ago.

Jaime considers that SE tends to grow and become more diverse if it gains representativeness in other islands, even though it is predominantly present in São Miguel. He asks directly what I want to know, and I start by asking about the origin of SE in the Azores. Jaime asks if I will go to the institutions. When I nod positively, he says that maybe I would better do it first and then go back to IAS to talk about it. I explain that I went to talk to him first, given that the people I spoke to remember his name as someone important related to the concept.

I find his reluctancy to speak strange, albeit in a general way, about SE on the island, given that he agreed to schedule the conversation for this purpose. Jaime does not seem very willing to share his experiences and his face shows a man who is not at ease.

Jaime proposes that we draw up a joint plan for the investigation. He says that questions like the ones I asked do not come up so often and that, therefore, he was not expecting that. Jaime comments that the stories

---

16   For example, the rooms in which management occupants work are at the top of the building and with the most beautiful views of the landscape, while public service is provided on the ground floor. To deepen this theme of architecture as a symbol and build hierarchies and values, it is worth reading: FOUCAULT, M. Vigiar e Punir: o Nascimento da prisão. Petrópolis: Vozes, 2005.

of SE on the island do not appear overnight and that to recover them is complicated.

I then ask about public policies related to SE, in addition to which organizations he and the IAS consider to be SE. Jaime says that a mapping is being carried out by the IAS to better understand what SE organizations on the island do. During his speech, he mixes the terms Solidarity Economy and Social Economy. Sometimes he stutters and talks about Social Economy and then 'corrects' for Solidarity Economy.

Mariléia says that the SE mapping in the Azores is being carried out as follows: delivering a questionnaire with a set amount of questions for organizations to answer, to get to know them. As they got to know these 'companies', they requested some documentation that Cresaçor did not have. The term Mariléia uses to describe the initiatives: companies, as well as the relationship with Cresaçor and the way used to carry out the mapping, is noteworthy. But what does Cresaçor have to do with the mapping of the Regional Government of the Azores?

I ask if they have only visited organizations which are already affiliated with Cresaçor and Mariléia replies affirmatively: *"only the members of the Cresaçor list, the cooperative which are members of Cresaçor"*. Noting my expression of surprise, she comments that the mapping was done only between these organizations, but that perhaps this is not the most correct, considering that there may be other 'companies' and projects.

I ask how to join Cresaçor since public policies are aligned only with the cooperatives that are part of it. They say that there are no pre-defined criteria, but that alignment is necessary. In Jaime's opinion, Cresaçor would bring a concern for quality certification, which many people do not have when they decide to work collectively.

Jaime says that Rosa Amparo helped in the elaboration of the questionnaire used by the IAS to collect data about SE organizations and Mariléia adds that indicators provided by that professor were used, based on her theoretical definitions of what would be the SE: *"the questionnaire has already been delivered to all companies and we are now looking forward to receiving the requested documentation"*.

I ask how it works, then, to map organizations that are not within the scope of Cresaçor, but I do not have a satisfactory answer, neither from Jaime nor from Mariléia, who just look at each other. Jaime says that I can go to organizations, that there is no problem with that, and that the initial focus of SE in the Azores was the training of young people with disabilities. At times, he treats SE as a 'job placement', with a transitory character, which would have the ultimate goal of inserting people into 'normal' jobs in the private sector. Jaime seems impatient to end the conversation. Carlos and Mariléia look more helpful and open.

Finally, I comment that Maurício Tinoco mentioned about an association of deaf women, located in Lagoa, which in his memory would be the first Solidarity Economy organization on the island. He replies that the co-op name is Megasil, initially led by Letícia Moura, Santa Casa Mercy director at that time. He admits he does not know what has happened to the cooperative since its foundation, *"many years ago"*. He also says that this cooperative has never *"officially"* entered the Solidarity Economy field, *"not even as a Private Social Solidarity Institution"* (IPSS).

But what does an IPSS consist of? What links can it have to the Solidarity Economy?

Summary about IPSS and conversation with Carlos Bastos

According to the Portuguese Social Security, a IPSS "aims to exercise social action in the prevention and support in different situations of fragility, exclusion or human need, promoting social inclusion and integration"[17].

The IPSS statute was approved by Decree-Law number 119/83, on 25 February 1983, and these initiatives are not for profit. Their objectives include the provision of goods and services related to the support of children and young people, families, protection of the elderly and invalids in situations of lack or reduction of subsistence means or capacity for work, education and professional training of citizens, housing problems, health promotion and protection, among others.

What happens when an organization is recognized as an IPSS in everyday practice? According to the legislation, once registered, it acquires the status of "public utility company, resulting from the State's attribution of benefits (tax exemptions, financial support) and charges (accountability, obligation cooperation with the Public Administration)" . However, it is noteworthy that the description of these benefits and charges is not present in the legal documents[18].

---

17   Segurança Social. IPSS/Iniciativas dos Particulares. 2008. Available at: http://195.245.197.202/left.asp?01.03. Accessed on: 19 may 2009.

18   Idem.

Cooperatives are not part of the legal form assumed by the IPSS status but can be approved if recognized as meeting the required criteria by the General Directorate of Social Security. According to current legislation,

> social solidarity cooperatives that pursue the objectives set out in the IPSS statute may request recognition of this quality from the Director-General of Social Security, to assimilate those institutions and apply the same statute of rights, duties, and benefits, namely tax[19].

The possibility that cooperatives are recognized as IPSS only became real as of January 15, 1998, with the promulgation of Decree-Law number 7/98, which regulated the legal regime of social solidarity cooperatives, as well as the Law number 101/97 of September 13, 1997, which extended the rights, duties, and benefits of IPSS to social solidarity cooperatives.

An interesting fact is that "44.3% of the IPSS 's are from the Catholic Church, 20.7% from Actions, Plans or Projects for Local Development, 18% from other religious institutions and 17% from Associations (cooperatives, residents' associations, among others)"[20],[21]. What can be inferred is that a surprising 62.3% of IPSS come from entities linked to religious institutions, in which mercies are included.

Among the disadvantages of the IPSS status[22], there is a possible "strong financial dependence on the State, which [...] can lead to the loss of autonomy and the distortion of the principles of these organizations, the lack of a democratic tradition and a culture of participation within the organizations themselves (that is, disrespecting the maxim of 'one man, one vote')"[23].

Legislation and references explain a little about IPSS but do not address how these issues work daily. The legislation speaks of tax benefits as rights and accountability as a duty, but I do not understand what this means in practical terms. I need to say I found it very difficult to understand the information related to the process of requesting IPSS status.

One of the requirements is that the request is submitted by the members

---

19   Idem.

20   HOVEN, R. v. d. Social work and the third sector in Portugal. Available at. http://cms.euromodule.com/servlet/PB/-s/1xnvo1o1cbuuyh1kjgtnn9y9cijjlx9g4/show/1027649/po3rd_1.pdf. Accessed on: 10 may 2010. 2003.

21   SOUSA, G. M. F. d. As IPSS's, seu lugar em Portugal. Lisboa: Instituto Superior de Ciências do Trabalho e da Empresa, 2009.

22   Idem.

23   Idem

of the bodies that represent the cooperatives. My first understanding I had was that there would be external bodies to the cooperative, representative bodies of cooperatives, that should make the request. On May 22, 2009, I talk to Carlos Bastos at IAS to better understand how the IPSS scenario happen in the Azores.

I ask Carlos about the issue of external bodies requesting IPSS status to a cooperative. He explains that they are not external bodies, but the directors or president of the cooperative, according to its statute:

> the management makes executive decisions ... usually, this type of decision, although previously sanctioned by the cooperative assembly ... it is the management that formalizes ... I mean ... I, the president of the cooperative, I request this, this ... if in the statute you say that you have to be the president, the vice president to sign ... the statutes define the powers ... there is something here that is very important ... which is to realize in these situations that the institutions that are Social Security partners in the Solidarity Economy are employers ... they have a staff ... and the viability of the Social Security financial support ends up being limited to the existence of people to be integrated ... if I have a diagnosis of 20 people with problems, ready ... I speak about 20 ... what is my goal? Is it giving them jobs or giving them skills for them, with more difficulty, less difficulty, to integrate into the normal labor market? I am not going to be 100% successful ... but maybe my goal would be to have it because I should be working with women, but I should be working with companies ... I am training ... companies exist.

At this point, more clues that, at least in some organizations, there may be a separation between the direction and presidency of a cooperative and its workers, also in the Azores.

Another thing that deserves to be stressed is the vision of the Solidarity Economy in the Azores as having a temporary character as training people for the existing labor market in corporations. This is present in Carlos' speech, as well as recurring in several of the conversations that are part of the experiences already shared in this book.

Carlos comments that many institutions only ask for IPSS status to receive a refund of the Value Added Tax (VAT) when they execute a job or acquire a good. He comments that if one day these organizations need money to increase facilities, for example, they can also present a request with this aim since they have an IPSS status.

The fact that an organization is an IPSS (or have an IPSS status) gives access to financing funds, but prevents, on the other hand, organizations from competing for certain lines of financial incentive that the Regional Secretariat of Economy has. Carlos points out that to have the economic support of the IAS, an IPSS needs to establish a bilateral agreement with the government agency, which can allow the financing of administrative personnel, equipment, supplies, among other items.

Provisional reflections

Two things worry me about the 'mapping' carried out by IAS. The first is the way how it is done. A form is prepared, and a letter is sent to organizations beforehand to let them know that the IAS is going to visit them and that they need someone to receive them. This seems to me, at the very least, an approach that intimidates these organizations.

There is not even space to talk to its members, in addition to not showing any kind of sensitivity to understand their realities. There is no such desire, at least in those who designed the mapping. The intention is only for organizations to return completed forms, along with other documents requested by IAS.

The second thing that worries me is the fact that IAS conducts a mapping of SE on the island only with the cooperatives that are members of Cresaçor. Would not mapping be synonymous with seeking to discover and to know organizations?

What the IAS regards as mapping, in practice, is an investigation of organizations that have been already mapped and are affiliated to a cooperative linked to Jaime Marins and Ronaldo Rosa Amparo. Why?

Therefore, it seems essential to underline that only Cresaçor members are recognized as belonging to 'Solidarity Economy' according to the Regional Government of the Azores.

Associations and cooperatives that do not fall within Cresaçor are often invisible to IAS, that is, to the Government of the Azores, at least concerning public policies for SE. And this is in line with what I learned when I heard at UAC that Cresaçor is the one who operationalizes SE policies in the Azores.

This is not enough. Even though I managed to draw, albeit in general lines, some of the relationships that cross the concept of Solidarity Economy in the Azores, this does not comfort me. Just the other way around. I seek the new. The invention. The potential. In this sense, I am more interested in finding organizations that were not necessarily created 'top-down'.

I need to find organizations that may not have such close relationships with professional academics and members of the government to the point of being considered as the sole recipients of a mapping carried out to map what was already known beforehand.

Where is the life that overflows? Is there an example of an association or cooperative that is not trapped within these circles?

Where is the collective mobilization of people who fight for values such as egalitarianism, solidarity, and self-management in their organizations? Organizations in which the members are associated, members, owners, and in which they actively participate. Organizations where values such as those mentioned in interpersonal relationships thrive and which are not designed and thought by some and daily developed by others. Could Megasil be a concrete example?

V
MEGASIL
COOPERATIVE

It is May 14, 2009, and I am accompanied by Luciana, a student of the master's in Social and Solidarity Economy coordinated by Ronaldo Rosa Amparo. I first met her in one of my attempts to schedule an interview with this professor. Also interested in learning about SE initiatives on Portuguese soil, Luciana accepted my invitation to participate with me in this cartography on São Miguel Island, to experience Solidarity Economy outside the classrooms.

Finding Megasil

Based indications that Megasil was formally founded by Letícia Moura, a social worker and former deputy who supposedly worked at *Santa Casa Mercy* in Lagoa, Luciana and I head to Lagoa municipality, on an investigative mission in search of finding out more about the still unknown women's cooperative.

Upon arriving in Lagoa, about fifteen kilometers (almost 10 miles) from Ponta Delgada, the island's capital, we ask several people in almost empty streets where Santa Casa is. After some indications, it is not difficult to locate the institution's building, on the left side of a very narrow street in which cars are parked on the same side.

Entering the building, with nobody at the reception, we go to one of the doors in search of information and a lady comes towards us, asking what takes us there. I explain that we came from Lisbon and that we would like to know about a cooperative called Megasil. She says she knows it and thinks it still works, commenting that the co-op sells Portuguese sweet bread, cookies, and homemade bread. She asks me if I want to know where it is located. I nod affirmatively, since we had heard that it was one of the first cooperatives to be constituted on the Island:

> What I can tell you is this: are you driving? So, it is like that, you follow this street and you, therefore, turn in that tree ... even here on your left, you stop for the car and there is the fountain there. Stop the car and go down the stairs. And this little store that is on our left, Dona Andrea... this lady belongs to Megasil and she is the most accurate who can give you information about everything you want to know.

We leave Santa Casa Mercy and go to the indicated fountain. It is not difficult to find it, nor is the shop, a kind of mini market, located right in front of a church. I notice how people on the streets look at me and Luciana as if they want to know what we want. They note that we are not locals and, as in several small towns where everyone knows each other, the presence of strangers is quickly identified, and the target of curiosity[1].

When we arrive at the market, we enter and notice that, in addition to the basic products, typical regional items are also sold. We decide to take some to the cashier, to establish the first contact. We are attended by a lady who appear non-speaking, but who demonstrates being able to listen to us. We ask her and another girl who at her side who Andrea is. Smiling, this other woman says that she is herself, and I reply that we have reached the right person.

Luciana says she came from the continent and that I came from Brazil to talk to her. Andrea replies that she was *"looking at us suspiciously"* while we were walking through the products and Luciana tells her she can believe that it is for a good reason.

We come looking for information because we really want to know Megasil. We arrived in Lagoa without knowing anyone and then we went to Santa Casa Mercy. They told us to come here and look for Andrea, since she would be the right person to help us.

---

1   ELIAS, N.; SCOTSON, J. L. Os estabelecidos e os outsiders: sociologia das relações de poder a partir de uma pequena comunidade. Rio de Janeiro: Jorge Zahar Ed., 2000.

Andrea listens quietly, with that same suspicious look that she confessed moments before, and says: *"yes, I am all ears"*. We did not know where you were located or even if you still existed, I say.

Luciana says she is doing a master's degree and that I am doing a Ph.D. I explain that we are looking to learn about Portuguese associations and cooperatives and that we have heard that Megasil would be one of the oldest on the island.

Andrea confirms and says that Megasil is a 22-year-old non-profit cooperative. She also says that the girl next to her is Nesia, and adds:

> The first president [of the cooperative] was my mother-in-law, who is Nesia's mother. Nesia works there, but now she had an operation on her tendons and is on medical leave. She works hard because she has been there since the beginning, since 1988. I don't know if they know, but Megasil mainly employs disabled people. She [Nesia] is hearing-impaired. We have another one who is also hearing-impaired, Emanuela.

Andrea explains that some women founded Megasil, whose name derives from the initials of the names of the first members: *"M from Marina Emanuela, G from Greta... the very name Megasil has its history"*.

One of the main reasons for collective mobilization in the form of a cooperative was that some hearing-impaired women left school and had nowhere to go or what to do. Andrea explains that Megasil was founded because there was a need, in a way, to find a future for the hearing-impaired, to keep them occupied, since they left the special school around the age of 14 or 15 and had nothing to do or where to work.

"Thank God they are learning to be independent" says Andrea, pointing out that Nesia was in a special school, but that the Government stopped offering this service more than five years ago.

I realize that Megasil has emerged as a work and socialization space for women, some of whom were disabled right from the beginning. And more. Apparently, it was based on collective mobilization and not a 'top-down' initiative.

Luciana asks if the group of Megasil members all is made up of hearing-impaired people. *"No"*, I have been part of Megasil for some years, but that Bianca has been there since the beginning: *"[Megasil] is a son for her, she founded it, and helped to raise, to grow. There are thirteen co-workers, thirteen owners. Virtually all of them belong to the cooperative, that is, that is all of them"*.

In the beginning, they did not even have a space to call it their own and worked for almost three years in an old house that belonged to the municipality. Only then, with the help of the local government, they were able to acquire the building where they are today, which they have been paying in monthly installments over the years, with their own work's revenue.

Bianca works with the disabled in production processes and issuing invoices for customers, being the main responsible for the organization. Andrea is the president, secretary, treasurer, and in a way, she is also responsible for solving almost all administrative tasks.

Andrea reveals that, in addition to Megasil, she also works in this market where we are, an inheritance from her husband's family. "*I already gave Megasil's summary. Now go on*" she says, interested in knowing more about what we do there. Still intrigued, she asks:

> But how did you get to Megasil? Because we are small ... we do not advertise... maybe the work needed to be disclosed... I have been there for eleven years... sometimes there are difficulties... I cannot dedicate myself more, I have three children. I can't stretch... many associations have support from the Regional Government, but we don't. We just had the support of the municipality in our beginning and we've been here for 22 years.

I agree with Andrea and say that I see organizations that the Government started, that is, that came from 'top to the bottom', but I remind her that we are interested in knowing examples that were not constituted by the governmental initiative. I tell her that this initial mobilization of Megasil has great value. I explain that we went to the Institute for Social Action and that they know the initiatives they support, but they do not know so much about others. These are the places we must go to; I say. These examples are the ones we most need to look at, to know, to feel, to live, and, mainly, to listen, I continue.

I tell her that I see many initiatives that the government considers as Solidarity Economy in the Azores since I arrived, but that I learned about Megasil almost by accident, since IAS employees did not know how the cooperative was and if it still existed. But why didn't they know?

Andrea says:

> even five years ago we almost closed the doors, because the difficulties were many, we had not yet managed to sell our products in Modelo (supermarket) and unfortunately, we left our products in mini markets and we had a big drop in sales. It took us almost two years to

get our products into Modelo. We managed to get in[2].

Andrea says that Megasil essentially produces cookies: coconut, homemade, carrilho (corn), in addition to Portuguese sweet bread and, twice a week, homemade bread. But she warns that now they are not making bread, as they have a damaged oven whose spare part needs to come from the continent.

Luciana asks if Andrea has heard of Solidarity Economy and Andrea says no. Luciana says that she met me in Lisbon and reinforces that we came from Lisbon here to listen to people. We came to be able to hear and live a little of these associations and cooperatives, because in Lisbon we do not find examples like this, I complement. I speak of my stories in Brazil, and of my research with scavengers in Porto Alegre. I ask if she understands why we came from Lisbon and I leave her free to ask anything she wants. Andrea answers what she thinks:

> This is a joke. I was thinking that nowadays it no longer existed. Your beliefs, your conviction. Every time we see everything more materialistic, more selfish, more for power. I stopped watching it myself... I don't like to see soap operas, I don't see news, I stopped watching, I can't stand Socrates... I like fantasy films... at least I know it doesn't exist in the world, it will never happen... I prefer to see fantasies.... the little ones (people, organizations) getting smaller and smaller... the Government is giving more and more to a few... the big ones getting more and more money... This is faith... this is self-will, this is willpower.

We are anxious and want to know if we can go to Megasil to get to know the organization up close. Andrea says yes, recommending that we talk to Bianca and that she won't be bothered: *"she, more than anyone, is the person who has always helped and still works today, at night, and if it weren't for her sweat the door would already be closed. However, it is her sweat that is there, and she is the best person to speak from the beginning"*.

I get a little shy about going directly to Megasil and ask Andrea if she could speak to Bianca before. We do not want to go at a bad time. If we come on Monday, do you think it is a good day? Thoughtful and showing a suspicious face again, Andrea picks up the phone and calls Bianca:

> Dona Bianca, are you going to miss Monday? It's because I need to go there... I have two inspectors on Monday (laughing)... yes, yes, in the

---

> morning. There are two students. They met Megasil, heard about it, they gave indications and are doing their thesis, a study on Megasil... they wanted to know, to know from the beginning, you can say... it's nothing, don't worry... they want to know from the beginning, as it is was formed, this whole story... you have been longer than me... I have there for only 11 years.

Since Monday is a public holiday, we schedule it for Tuesday morning.

Tuesday, May 19, 2009.

I am afraid that arriving at Megasil for the first time will be difficult. I am afraid they will look at us with suspicion, mainly due to what I heard on Andrea's call to Bianca. Are they open to us? I leave Luciana at Megasil's door, help her get into the cooperative due to her fractured foot, and then park in the street.

A very good smell takes over the street that gives access to Megasil. A lady with gray hair says that

> the cookies are Megasil's pagan[3], and people without the pagan do nothing, right? The pagan is your little feet .... a cup without the foot is not standing... the cookies are the pagan's cup. Without the foot, the bowl cannot hold. So, if I stop making the cookies, Megasil will close. We don't want Megasil to close, so we always make cookies.

Andrea comes close to us and says that she doesn't know if she introduced herself, but that the person we talked to is Bianca, who has been there since the beginning, *"our mother, Megasil's mother"*. Bianca continues: *"Do you want to start with the office?"*. You are in charge, I answer. Bianca takes us to visit the facilities of Megasil Cooperative. And then Bianca asks: *"and you don't know what they want to know to start with. Do you want to know how it started? Please. Come with me..."*.

Megasil cooperative: a brief history

Andrea comments, during the first visit, that the name Megasil represents the initials of some of the people who were in the group that formed the organization, as she had already said when we were in her market. Bianca complements and explains that it is a conjunction of names such as Maristela, Emanuela, Gentil (her husband's surname), Zilá, among others.

Bianca takes us to Megasil's office, where the invoices for sold products are issued, as well as the receipts issued by the cooperative's suppliers. The

---

3   What sustains the cooperative. Its most significant source of income.

space is small, consisting of a wooden table on which you can see a computer and a calculator, in addition to an iron cabinet and two chairs.

Marina Bianca opens the iron closet doors and takes two large rolls of cardboard, rolled up and tied by rubber bands. She carefully opens and unrolls the cards to show us. Both are drawn and written by hand and she proudly says: "*here Megasil's history goes, from the beginning... it's already very old... here's the story... I did it... my authorship*".

On the cards you can read:

Megasil cooperative was born a while ago
Thanks to social services assistant Letícia Moura
Megasil cooperative must sound happy
To give work and support to the disabled brother
We all get along very well
We treat them all as equals
So that you never feel like an abnormal person
Work and play we share equally
We ask God for health and strength to always help us
We have already had the support of local and regional entities
God wish that in the future they will help us more and more
We have even been accepted by the new European Economic Community
Look... everyone supports us... nobody turns us down...
We hope that in the future more and more
Helping the disabled to feel like normal people
We ask the government for money to pay in installments
To buy our facilities
The facilities are old, we need to fix
We have the support of social equipment
We have already asked the Chamber, the President
He said in turn that what he could do
We were also invited to Lagoa fair
Look at the competence just because we are good people
Our products are good, well accepted in the market
They are all very tasty and very inexpensive
We were very willing to get it all
But we worked for many months without receiving a shield
It was not easy to get husbands to let us work
It was necessary to know how to ask and even make promises
The promise was not great, but it was willingly
It was made to the Divine Holy Spirit and the Holy Trinity
It is with a lot of work and with a lot of sacrifices
As many people know, we have many children
We are not professionals, we are just experienced
But we know how to please our disabled brothers

Upon hearing it and viewing the written verses on the cards, I live a little glimpse of the cooperative's history. It is possible to feel Bianca's emotion when remembering moments which she shared with the other members.

I say that it is very interesting to keep this 'piece of history', carefully written: *"one day I was at my house and things started to come. I was washing clothes... that inspires me a lot"*, she says, laughing a lot. Bianca says that Nesia, hearing-impaired and non-speaking, and another girl, diagnosed as schizophrenic, were at home without activities after completing school, as Andrea had already mentioned. Their mothers took the initiative to go and talk to a social worker, Letícia Moura, to see what they could do, since it was very difficult to find them a job. Together, Letícia, Bianca, and the others started to build the cooperative. In Bianca's words:

> We were in my house in the afternoon, in July... end of July, 1987... washing clothes, by the way, Maristela slammed the door... she lived on my street a little further down and called me. I met Zilá's mother, you don't know Zilá, there with them... and Nésia's mother, Andrea's sister-in-law. They went after Letícia to find them a job since they studied at the special school and their school time was over. That was when cooperatives came up, when I heard about cooperatives and remembered to create a cooperative to integrate the disabled. But they needed people to work with them. I didn't know how much I was going to generate income. I didn't even know if I was going to be able to generate any money. I said yes without knowing. I wanted to work and that's how it happened.

The idea of working with cookies was not immediate: *"we didn't know what we could do. We were lucky"*. It is interesting to pay attention to hear them say they were lucky, while deciding to face a challenge and create the cooperative with the disabled, start working with food, making cookies and cakes.

Uncertainties did not paralyze them. On the contrary, they served as an impulse to invent and implement possibilities, to dive into the unknown, to experiment, to live. With a serene, calm look, Bianca tells another part of her trajectory:

> Okay, we tried it. We started there at the Parish Council of Santa Cruz... I don't know if you already knew, which is down here on the street... the president at the time lent us the kitchen. There was a kitchen here, he lent it and we went there to make cookies. Nobody was a professional and to we took the necessary utensils from our homes so we could begin. I took a pan, another one took a spade... we took kitchen things to try... Nesia, another girl, me, and my cousin who is no longer there.

Megasil started in August 1987, not yet a "real deal", but to first become a job for these women. The organization did not start with the intention of making serious money from selling products. Bianca explains:

> it was to sell, but it was like a little thing... who wanted to buy? And to entertain those girls. Then we started those stores up here... take and try... try... some don't wanted because they were disabled... we made cakes, put them in a bag, ten to one side, ten to the other... and Nesia took part to one side, and Zilá to the other, they did it the distribution... and we got here... we are on the way.

Bianca had five children at the time, who went to Megasil with her mother, since there was no one else to take care of them: *"we started like this. Then we grew up, enjoying it and we've been here for 22 years"*.

In the beginning, they worked for many months without receiving anything, since what they managed to produce was sold in small markets in the region and the revenue was only sufficient to buy the supplies. When there was some money left, they bought kitchen utensils and, little by little, stopped using the equipment they took from their homes.

Bianca's learning was also progressive in the sense of working and communicating with people who, according to the dominant standards, had communication and expression difficulties, such as people diagnosed as disabled and/or schizophrenic. She comments that these processes were not easy, requiring a lot of willpower. In the beginning, she had even more difficulties to understand and be understood by hearing-impaired Megasil members than today: *"in the beginning, it was just 'uh uh uh' and hand movements. First, we had to understand what they were saying. Nowadays I talk to Nesia and Emanuela without any problem, and they too"*.

As an organization that works with food, Megasil cannot receive people who have diseases that cause secretions or skin problems, and, for this reason, they end up with hearing-impaired people and people with mental disorders. Zilá, one of the members of the initial group, has already had to leave Megasil because she started having problems with her hands skin.

Bianca, citing the example of Nesia, who she considers to be very smart, attentive, and always looking to getting things done, takes the opportunity to unmask the idea of those who consider the disabled as incapable people. All people are treated as equals: *"the way we always treated everybody... not treating them differently because they are disabled... they want to do everything we do... tell the soap operas, talk, tell what they saw over the weekend, that's why they feel very good here"*.

It is noteworthy that, at that time, work was only part-time, for a few hours in the afternoon. They started making cookies, milk cakes and other recipes learned from the participants' mothers. They also made Portuguese sweet bread with the same recipe that they still produce and sell today, but they cooked everything in the ovens of two industrial stoves powered by gas:

> The first ovens we had were offered from a nursing home in Ponta Delgada that closed. The stove was no longer in good condition, but it was good for us because we had nothing, right? And then two of those stoves came from home. So, we started to bake dough and bread and cookies... all in those ovens.

Bianca says they talked to many people to find out if they were interested in joining the cooperative, but most of them wanted to know the salary they would receive in advance. She repeats, with a certain tone of criticism, that no one else wanted to join the cause for not knowing how much one was going to earn. Concerning the disabled, Megasil had up to seventy people working together in the borrowed kitchen.

Bianca has four siblings and says that it was difficult during her childhood and adolescence because she liked to study, but her family did not let her study afraid that she would 'get lost' in life, *"even more as a woman"*. She worked sewing at home when she was still single, but that was not what she liked since she always wanted to work outside, while her mother and father did not want that:

> I couldn't work, but there were always some little opportunities. They needed a woman for this or that, a store, but my parents and my husband never wanted me to go... and then it's like this... to be continuous in a school... I wanted to learn to be a hairdresser and my husband didn't want to... hairdresser... it wasn't a profession seen like that... do you understand? However, with five children... I had all but Greta, this opportunity from Megasil... I wanted nothing more... I said I will...

Bianca says that she wanted to work abroad for years, although she never did that. Even after she was married, this desire remained. However, she affirms her husband would not let her and did not want her to work outside the home: *"it was not easy to get it. I always worked alone; it was for my life. But I wanted to try it. I'm going to experience what it's like to work outside"*, she says, confessing that she had to fight *"a little bit"* with her husband so that she could put her will into practice.

She reaffirms that she went to Megasil *"by luck. I said well we will try it because I had never worked and said I will try it and look... we are never disappointed;*

we always take this forward". Bianca comments that the husbands of other members also had the same attitude as hers, which made this another link of affinity between them.

Marina Bianca's speech and attitudes illustrate an interesting point: Megasil started not only to generate work and income for some women with hearing loss and schizophrenia, but also on the initiative of women who wanted to work outside.

Bianca says that at the beginning her husband did not want to, but that today he is the only man in the cooperative and responsible for distributing the products at the most different points of sale. She explains that when she started working at Megasil, she did everything until she convinced him to go to work with her: "*if I came alone, I would be at odds, so I said: let's go both. To start the cooperative, we needed 13 cooperatives. We had 3 disabled people and we had to have their tutors. [My husband] He came with me and stayed. We started to work together*".

If Megasil took its first steps in August 1987, it was only in late 1988 and early 1989 that the cooperative moved to the building where it is today. They asked for government assistance to buy the building, but they only got a loan. I am surprised that the building of the cooperative is already owned by them and paid for with their work. Bianca comments:

> It is ours! We borrowed money from the government to avoid paying interest and at the time he lent it to us. It was 5000 of the old currency. 2000 was lost and the other 3000 we were paying in installments... every month we paid X... that was in the Financial Management Office... and only then when we came here to this house, we bought an electric oven that is there, that you will see. He's not sure how old he is.

Bianca comments that, with the passage of time and the increase in production and sales, the cooperative became better structured. An electric oven was purchased with the cooperative's income, paying in installments with the sales revenue of the products they manufactured.

Andrea does not speak much with us on this visit and acknowledges: "*I don't like being in the spotlight*". She says Megasil has always faced many difficulties and that, despite the countless problems they faced, they were not always looking for help and that, many times, she and Bianca suffered, alone, without disclosing what was happening. Andrea recognizes that if they sought help first, they could solve some problems before they got worse.

About 3 years ago, the update of hygiene rules regarding Hazard Analysis and Critical Control Points (HACCP), represented one of the biggest challenges in Megasil's history. Some of the buyers of Megasil's products suddenly demanded this certification. According to Andrea, things reached a level where they could no longer continue without help: *"either we go somewhere, or the door will close"*. In this episode, Megasil received a letter with all the items they needed to implement, with a very tight deadline:

> We had to ask for help, we didn't have any money. We had to pay for technicians, expenses, we had to do works... that was when we went to the [Municipal] Chamber. There was an association to support rural development and we competed. We made a budget, we did the works, we had to go to the bank to ask for money and other things were discovered during the work. The budget was not enough. We asked for a five-year short-term credit, but we didn't know that we could use any specific credit, government programs. I was already waiting, the suppliers were all waiting, we were out of time.

Andrea thinks that they were successful due to the support of wealthy and influential people in the Autonomous Region. She explains that the credit they obtained from the bank (to complete the amount of the subsidy) was secured by her husband (owner of the market in which she works), Marina de Letícia and Marina dos Anjos.

These last two belong to the cooperative's management board in formal terms, in the statute, but they never really worked with them. They are people with a good financial situation, who are part of the cooperative in their statutes but do not actually work in the organization. In this episode, the two lent their names to Megasil to facilitate its access to credit, which is valued by Andrea:

> They gave a lot of votes of confidence and never said no. I explained what had to be done, decided, signed the papers and that's it. They never said no. I have Megasil's checks that must be signed by her. I am in control; the checks are signed with me and she never suspected. I have held meetings sometimes with them more to give news, but, despite all this, they have given me every vote of confidence.

I realize, once again, the importance of trust in interpersonal relationships between them, reinforced at various times in the cooperative's history.

Andrea comments that, since always, they are unaware of most of the government support available: *"a subsidy like this, but I don't know. We don't know how it works... Only public entities do. Does not reach normal citizens"*. She raises a very interesting question that runs through Megasil's history: the distance between the Government and its citizens, especially concerning the access to funding by small organizations without great political influence. Bianca, like Andrea, says that she also does not have much knowledge about certain things, referring to the government support mentioned.

With the financial support of the Economy Secretariat of Azores Regional Government, Megasil have acquired another furnace. Bianca considers that this support occurred, in part, because Letícia helped with her influence in the state agency.

Andrea considers that there is a lack of information on the part of Megasil members. In the beginning, they had many government visits, perhaps because Letícia was "in that environment", knowing about government protocols and always taking the information to Megasil. *"But she has her life there, right?"*, Says Andrea. Intrigued, we asked if Letícia is still part of Megasil, and Andrea says yes. When we asked if there was a problem between them, we heard: *"she went to live her life, she is very busy. We have solved things, and when we are very distressed, we turn to her"*.

Letícia still officially belongs to Megasil management, but only in the statutes. Andrea says that she *"has another life already"* and that she once said to them: *"you are already on your own... you already know how to do everything on your own, now get on with it"*. Andrea recognizes that the social worker helped the cooperative a lot in the beginning and that, now, she works in a Youth home, while her husband, who was once Megasil's president even though he never worked there, is the provider of Santa Casa Mercy.

Would it be interesting, then, to hear a little bit of Megasil's story from Letícia herself?

On June 3, 2009, we went to Megasil initially to find out about them on how to find Letícia, since we would like to know more about the beginning of the cooperative and her work with the girls. However, on the way to the cooperative, I thought it would be more appropriate to first know from the organization current members their views on this possible conversation. Since we do not know about the story or possible fights and disagreements in the past, I considered that this posture would be a matter of respect for them. Before taking the initiative to speak with Letícia, what do Bianca and Andrea think about this possible conversation?

As we passed the corner of the cooperative's street, we noticed that a truck was obstructing the passage and so we decided to go first to talk to Andrea in her minimarket. When we got there, we noticed that she was busy receiving supplies and making payments. We waited for her to finish and then we told her that we went there to get her opinion on a possible conversation with Letícia. Andrea's facial expression is indescribable and reflects a mixture of reflection, concern, and no happiness or joy.

I tell her that I would like to know what she thinks about it, whether it is a good idea. She replies that she does not have an opinion, which is neutral, but I insist that her opinion is very important to us. After finishing delivering the checks to the respective suppliers, she accompanies me to the car, in which Luciana was waiting, due to her reduced mobility due to her fractured foot.

After talking a little about Luciana's surgery, we explained that Andrea's opinion is very important. I say that we would like to know, mainly, if she thought it would be interesting to go and talk to Letícia, or if she had had some kind of friction, disagreement, or something like that in the past: "*Some things we shouldn't say*".

Andrea had to do almost everything to prevent Megasil from closing the doors, struggling with difficulties of the most diverse types, including accounting, fines from the State finance department, among others. She recognizes that Bianca has great merit in keeping Megasil open for so long, since the first (Andrea) does not make a living from the cooperative, while the second does, with a withdrawal of around 300 euros per month, less than a minimum wage salary.

We feel that at this moment it is better not to look for Leticia, respecting Andrea's and Bianca's feelings. No one better than themselves to know what they have been through and what impacts our attitude could bring. The meeting with Letícia was left to another moment.

Andrea invites us to see the rest of the facilities and Bianca says that they have already made yogurt cakes at Megasil in the past, but that since the cookie is the cooperative's 'pagan', they were unable to keep all the things they wanted.

They introduce me to Emanuela, who looks seriously at me, almost angry. Her look is intimidating at times. Bianca says she had meningitis at the age of 10, but she understands everything we say and knows how to read her lips. I am also introduced to Maristela, who has no diagnosed physical or mental disability and works with them a few days a week, although she is no longer a Megasil member.

Andrea says goodbye and tells us to arrange the rest with Bianca. I am very grateful for her support and she says that we know where to find her in case we need anything else. I also thank Bianca for welcoming us with 'open arms'. She replies that we can come back when we want to since currently, they work from 9 am to 3 pm every day and, on Thursdays, also from 9 pm to 11 am on Friday, just to make the Portuguese sweet bread.

I am surprised by the length of the workday and say that I would like to see the work they do at night. Bianca says that we should come on Thursday night.

> At 9 pm I come and then we cook the bread. If you want to come, we will have company... you don't bother... you can come.

On the way out she gives us coconut cookies, homemade, and carrilho (corn) to take. "*Anyone who comes here is treated equally. Be old, be new, be rich, be poor*", says Bianca, when I thank her for treating us so carefully.

Megasil cooperative in 2009

Not all people who founded Megasil remain today. A sixteen-year-old girl, diagnosed with psychiatric disorders, has already worked with the cooperative, and was considered to be very aggressive. She went to work 'hitting' the dough so that she could discharge all her aggressiveness. Bianca says that this girl used to beat the dough as well or even better than the machines and stopped being so aggressive over time. A former participant has a disability pension due to tendonitis in her hands. Another, Beatriz, now works at the Modelo supermarket, as the income she earned at Megasil was not enough. And Zilá, who started with the group, but ended up with hands full of bubbles and was no longer able to continue working with food products.

Bianca says she understands when some workers leave the cooperative over time, because sometimes people need to rest or even end up retiring, and that she could never force someone to stay, but she says in a sad tone: "*sometimes it costs... sometimes it costs a little time... but that's it, sometimes I can't take it, right? It is life*".

As already mentioned, Megasil has people who are listed in the bylaws as members, but who do not work effectively in the cooperative: "*presence workers*". Among them are João and Letícia, who only participate in a few sporadic meetings, since they served to complete the required initial group: thirteen members were needed to officially register the cooperative.

Among those 'who make the cooperative happen' in its daily struggles, there are cooperative members who are workers, that is, who are listed in the statute as belonging to the cooperative - "*cooperative workers*" - and others who work there but who are not 'official' members of the organization.

Today, Bianca, Carolina, Andrea, Emanuela, Nesia (Andrea's sister-in-law), Maristela, and Fernando Gentil (Bianca's husband) are among the cooperative workers. Fernando is dedicated to the distribution of Megasil's products. He makes daily deliveries in his own car since the cooperative does not yet have a vehicle. Manoela, the goddaughter of Bianca, currently works only two or three times a week on the day shift.

Andrea's sister-in-law, Nesia, is deaf and is currently on sick leave due to arm pain, possibly due to tendonitis. Bianca says that she is the most agile and dexterous of all with the cookie dough, being fast, accurate, and often cutting the dough while talking to her colleagues, without even looking at the dough itself. Bianca, laughing, confesses that she has already tried to imitate her, with no success.

Emanuela, who is also deaf, takes care of the oven with great precision, alternating between shaping the cookies, placing the trays with the ones that are already formed and raw in the oven, and looking to avoid letting the baking ones burn. Besides, when watching her cutting and shaping the cookies, the skill with which she performs the movements is noteworthy.

On the first day I arrived at Megasil, Emanuela received me with an angry and serious face, but with the passing of the days and the consecutive meetings, she already smiles a lot, and talks about the pain in her knee. Bianca points out that the work developed at Megasil is taken seriously and that respect between everyone is essential for daily activities.

Carolina is the one who has been the least at Megasil, but she has a very close and friendly relationship with Bianca. She would have liked to have studied more and become a teacher: "*I have never been able to study as much as I would like. I liked it very much. I always have. I really liked school, that chalk smell... good thing. I enjoyed going to school so much*".

I ask Carolina why she has not been at Megasil since the beginning and she tells me that she was only invited by Bianca five years ago and that, since then, she accepted the invitation and has never left. The education of her children has always been a priority for her, who speaks proudly of how she feels about having a son who graduated as a lawyer and who remains a simple person today, treating everyone equally.

Carolina comments that the workload at Megasil has been progressively increasing due to the growing order volume. She says that she communicates with Bianca many times without even speaking: "*I and Bianca speak in parables, without even opening my mouth, just by looking at each other. No one understands anything*". Bianca adds by saying that for a good connoisseur, half a word is enough.

I ask Bianca why she has such a close relationship and such complicity with Carolina, even when she needs to 'hold the bar' since both are very supportive of each other. She says that because Carolina understood her, they ended up developing this relationship.

Lúcia, who has been an orphan since adolescence and has been diagnosed with psychiatric problems, has also worked in Megasil for many years. Bianca says that she always needs to be "pulling" for her, telling her to do various tasks: *"she rolls the cookie, cuts it, rolls it again... she is sometimes rolling, and she doesn't even have her head on what she is doing... is far away"*. Lucia arrived at the cooperative indicated by a doctor. She was never paid with Megasil funds because she is part of a government's income program and receives the Guaranteed Minimum Income (RMG). Bianca considers that she is much better today than when she arrived at Megasil: more active, smart, and communicative.

In the beginning, neither Bianca nor Andrea imagined that the cooperative would develop and last for so many years. As time went by, some dreams were realized and new ones were built: *"we didn't even dream, not even far, that I was going to buy a house. We bought this property, who thought? At first, we didn't dream of buying the property, but now we dream of buying more... right?"*.

Reflective, Bianca goes on to say that if at the beginning they took even the culinary instruments from home, today they are already confident that they can get what they need from the work done: *"now if I need something, I will buy it. Although it is not much [what we earn] I already have the confidence that if I make a purchase, I will have to work to pay for it and I know that if I work, I will pay it"*.

Concerning the relations between people at Megasil, changes are also perceived, since *"in the beginning, there was not so much trust, companionship... today we are a family"*.

General assemblies take place whenever necessary, but they do not happen regularly, although they are fully aware that the statute expresses that regular meetings should take place throughout the year.

Megasil members do not earn a minimum wage, having monthly incomes of approximately 200 or 250 Euros, according to the cooperative's sales. Bianca receives a little more for having the responsibility of coordinating the entire production, in addition to so many other activities: *"they earn 200 and some change and I earn 300 and some change because I have this responsibility all around me. If I do wrong, I am responsible"*.

Social Security discounts are based on just 15 working days per month, due to a lack of financial resources. No one receives holiday or Christmas allowance, but if sales and revenues increase at the end of the year, the surpluses are divided among all. Andrea comments: *"We earn more, they have a little more. We earn less, they wait. We have our suppliers, our taxes, the Government does not wait, unfortunately, the Government does not wait, we have to pay"*.

It is worth mentioning, once again, that not all workers are remunerated by Megasil. Andrea receives absolutely nothing, zero. And others, like Lúcia, are paid directly by the RMG.

From the cooperative's sales, they pay the workers' income, funds for the payment of taxes, as well as other expenses such as water, electricity, oil, raw materials, garbage collection, among others.

Almost all Megasil members get their only income from the cooperative. Most work part-time, usually from nine in the morning to four in the afternoon. But the division of labor in the cooperative is complex.

As already explained in the previous section, Megasil regularly produces cookies - coconut, homemade, carrilho (corn) -, in addition to Portuguese sweet bread and, twice a week, homemade bread.

Due to the economic importance of cookies in the cooperative's recipes - they are Megasil's pagan, according to Bianca - during the aforementioned 'normal' work shift, mainly dedicated to production.

When the dough is made, in the early hours, the ladies who are deaf do not work, but only Bianca, Andrea, and Carolina. Lídia, Bianca's daughter, works for a few nights with the group, but this is not constant.

The heavy workload and the shortage of personnel end up overloading some members. Andrea comments that when Bianca is absent, things are almost impossible inside Megasil, as there is no one to replace her. Bianca admits and adds that she only leaves for two or three days a week when she takes a vacation: *"I do everything, from the office to cleaning... everything... if I need an invoice, I will come by. You have to answer the phone, I'm going to solve it"*.

We spent several nights working together. Talking. In most mornings, afternoons and especially in the evening, we talk not only about work, but also about loves, relationships, politics, and expectations about life.

It seems impossible to analyze work relationships at Megasil just as such, as they are crossed by many other feelings and dimensions. Bianca says:

> I feel like their mother and I do everything so that they... if I need
> to work more than they do, I work so that they don't get upset...
> Emanuela, you're going to do that and that... and she says that she
> can't... ok, I end up going to do it... I really like. I play with them, I sing,
> I do everything with them... sometimes they disrespect, they do not
> listen to anyone... but you see in my expression that I am bad, and she
> is soft, and in a little while, she comes to kiss me, to hug me... Bianca is
> good... I am bad sometimes... and only this fact that she recognizes... is
> how to say a mother is a mother... But this is how our story is.

It is very interesting to notice the way Bianca works the characteristics of each person. Not only she has an enormous creative capacity, but she also demonstrates her determination, and, above all, she believes and values others.

Although she gives more focus to the production processes, she also develops a lot of management errands, such as manual invoices, since she does not understand computer science. Only Andrea, Bianca, and Carolina participate in most cooperative's strategic decisions. Emanuela and Lúcia are not always able to understand what is going on and Bianca then sits down with them and explains everything in general terms: *"for them to understand certain things, they have to spend more time. You must stop, look, explain and there are certain things that, if not well explained, you are aware of some wrong things"*.

Some issues that cause conflicts at Megasil do not always appear clearly during the meetings. The fact that the other co-workers do not work late at night seems to cause some discomfort and a feeling of injustice for some, who comment that Emanuela *"participated in this other shift only once and then said that she would not come again because her husband did not want her to go home alone"*.

Income discrepancies within the cooperative can raise complaints in interpersonal relationships. Andrea comments that this is an obstacle for the entry of new people, mainly for administrative functions, since they do not want to bring someone who will earn more than the others.

Self-management is built, even with difficulties concerning the participation of everybody. Their will is visible in not letting the co-op lose its autonomy and also in not adopting unfair and/or unequal practices.

Andrea has some accounting basic notions and Megasil hires an accountant who, every two or three months, signs the cooperative's fiscal documents. She comments on her difficulty in carrying out administrative activities, given that she also works at her husband's market. She says she receives nothing for the work she does at Megasil:

> I, as I am in charge of everything, cannot make it... maybe I have lost a lot... because I need to walk, to know... and I am also busy here, I cannot give them what they need. I needed a person in the office to spread the word. I don't have time to do it all. I often do Megasil's things at night. Customers, suppliers, payments, accounting, I have often done at night. I was supposed to go once a week. I do and do not receive it. What I do, the responsibility I have at Megasil, I don't receive anything.

I notice that there is a certain difficulty for performing mathematical calculations, mainly on the part of Bianca, when a man arrives at the cooperative's window to buy 5 bags of biscuits. When it comes to informing the price to the boy, the difficulty in multiplying five by 2.30 euros is clear, the individual price of each package of the biscuit purchased by the man. And for very little the purchase did not come for 7.50 Euros.

After more than two months with one broken oven, finally the technician responsible for repairing it arrives at 11 pm, explaining that the piece had to come from Lisbon. After about thirty minutes the oven is in operation and Bianca and Carolina decide to take advantage of the day to make bread, in addition to the more than 120 large units of Portuguese sweet bread (one kilo each) and 95 small ones (500g each) that day. With the help of the electric kneader, they use forty kilograms of flour, which, together with the other ingredients, are enough for about forty-nine large pieces of bread and sixteen small ones.

The Portuguese sweet bread is sold for 2.50 Euros a kilo, and a one-kilo homemade bread for 1.20 Euros, due to differences in the cost of the ingredients of each product.

I comment that while shopping at an island market, I noticed that their cookies are the most expensive and the ones that are always in the least quantity on the shelves, compared to other brands. Carolina, speaking only to me, says that the price is higher because they use eggs, lard, butter, that is, traditional and quality ingredients, while other organizations use 'egg powder' and other lower quality raw materials to reduce the price.

I explain that I saw on the market the large sweet bread being sold for more than three Euros and Andrea, showing some surprise in discovering the sales value used, says: *"wow! They earn a lot of money... they earn a lot. Because they buy at 2.20 plus VAT, you know... and then they discount 12%... and they sell at three and such"*.

The markets discount a percentage of their cookie prices for promotional purposes, cards, among other things. But Megasil still consider it worthwhile to have its products in larger markets, such as Modelo and Sol e Mar, because of the large quantities they buy.

Modelo and Sol e Mar take a long time to pay Megasil, sometimes up to three months. Almost all suppliers pay a fee characterized as 'shelf rent' to have their products sold in these markets, but Bianca explains that Megasil has never paid this and will not pay:

> at the beginning when we asked our product to be sold there, we said once and for all that we didn't have the money to be able to pay, right, and what we could do was a discount. And that's what we do, but the other suppliers pay, make the discount as we do and have an employee there with the product on the shelf. We don't do that.

Bianca seizes the moment and talks about the relationships that big markets establish with their suppliers, explaining that in many cases products are given by the suppliers to be promoted in the markets and sold at promotional prices: *"they sent us fax asking what we were going to collaborate with a fair. We answered that we couldn't because we didn't have the financial conditions to do it"*.

She complements saying that Megasil's products do not need a promotion with customers, as they are always sold very quickly, mainly since they are homemade products, with natural ingredients: *"ours gets there and sells quickly... while the others stay in the shelves"*.

I am surprised by the type of relationship that Megasil has built with these retail giants and I ask how the initial negotiations went with Modelo and Sol e Mar. Bianca and Andrea tell me this rich story:

> we were always trying to contact Modelo, always, always. We tried to talk to the Mayor, to Letícia... and she knew someone... we had been trying for almost 2 years... [Bianca] I had to speak properly with the owner of the Modelo. She lived up here in Lagoa. I tried to contact her by phone, I sent bread, I sent cookies, I went with one of those girls who work with me. I went there to talk to her, to tell her that we had tried in every way to get into Modelo and that we couldn't, and clients who came from Sol e Mar, sometimes went to Modelo to ask if they didn't have Megasil's cookie, but Sol e Mar had. I had this whole conversation with the owner of Modelo. And then she told me she was going to put the cookies in there. So, I went with this man, I went to Ponta Delgada and there was the biscuit being sold at Modelo. And we've been after them for two years or more. They got it the first time, then they stopped asking for more... and then we walked and I went back to talking to this French lady... already on the phone, I told her that I didn't understand the reason why they had stopped buying... and

> I know they asked again. And by the way, Modelo is the market that buys more cookies from Megasil... more than Sol e Mar... the retailer that came last and buys more cookies.

Bianca, Carolina, and Andrea comment that homemade cookies are the ones that sell the most, followed by coconut cookies and, finally, carrilhos. The sweet bread arrives at Sol e Mar every Friday morning and does not take long to sell out, since there are customers who complain that they went in the afternoon or on the next day and did not find the product anymore.

I ask, curious, why they do not increase the number of doughs for this market, and Bianca gives me a lesson:

"because there are also other suppliers,

other qualities of doug.

Everyone has to win...

everyone has to sell...

everyone has to have their space".

For them, there is no objective of conquering the market for Megasil at the expense of the livelihood of other people and organizations, who also depend on their jobs to live.

There are also other problems for Megasil today: difficulties in meeting the orders they receive, mainly due to the lack of personnel. Bianca comments that they have already made cakes, among other recipes, but that they stopped doing it precisely because of a lack of workforce.

For producing 100 kilos of Portuguese sweet bread, 50 kilos of flour, and 19 kilos of sugar are used, in addition to other ingredients. The work begins in the late afternoon and, until evening, the dough grows. Only then do they fill the shapes, which will grow even more, before going to the oven. They throw flour over the dough when they put it to rest so as not to stick to the cloth it covers.

The work is tiring. Bianca and Carolina have their back hurt more than the legs. The ingredients take an hour to hit the mixer today, but Bianca confesses:

> I already knead a lot of dough in my hand. I've already kneaded a lot of dough just in bowls, twice, three times in a row, followed by ten kilos of flour. Because there (in the machine) it takes fifty kilos, but ten kilos of flour to knead by hand, in a pan like this... it's really kneaded.

Megasil's egg supplier has been the same for 22 years, that is, since the beginning. Sometimes, he stops receiving on time without complaining, hoping that they will have enough revenue to pay off debts, while still supplying the products: *"since we started, we have this same egg supplier... 22 years. He knows our situation and he can afford to wait a little bit. If he couldn't, he wouldn't. He started with us. The flour one is also like that, with us for many years"*.

They ask if I am not going to help. Carolina brings me a cap and an apron. I ask for help from Bianca, laughing. I dress to work with them, still shy and embarrassed. Luciana asks to start taking pictures with my camera. Ask everyone if they do not care to be on the pictures. None of them bothers. They call me to start working. I put on the apron to help them with the night shift.

Carolina tells me to follow her so I can start learning how to prepare the dough: *"take the dough... don't you? do it like that and cut yourself"*. It seems easy for her. I say that I will not have the agility that they have when taking it out of the bowl and placing it in aluminum molds. I try once. I fail. They all laugh at me. Instead of cutting a kilo of dough, the piece I cut must have, at most, seven hundred grams.

Both Bianca and Carolina try to help me. Carolina repeats the procedure several times. Bianca is further away taking care of the sink and the oven. I go back to watching Bianca and Carolina removing the dough from the basins, rolling it in her hand, weighing it, and placing it in the aluminum molds. The way they take the dough is fantastic. They dance with the dough in their hands.

I take and bring aluminum forms to and from one stainless steel table to another, and from the tables to the metal trays that go to the oven. Lídia explains to me that after the doughs are weighed and placed in the molds, they rest for more than an hour covered, then to cut an X-shape with the scissors on their top: *"for the dough to 'open' and look more beautiful when baked in the oven"*.

Carolina says that when she and Bianca are alone, there is no time for anything, because while one is doing one thing, the other is already doing another, and when they finish an activity, there is another to be started, barely giving time to wash the dishes.

We talk about loving relationships and the most diverse subjects. We exchange confessions that I prefer not to share, as a sign of respect for the trust that has been established between us. It is almost 2 in the morning.

Luciana has already returned to Lisbon to recover from a foot surgery and undergo physical therapy. On another dawn, I arrive at Megasil alone, being greeted by Carolina with great joy. She shows me pictures of her family so I can get to know her family members, her children, her husband, among others. Carolina proudly shows her son's wedding photos.

Early nights are full of mathematical operations. They spend a lot of time counting the cakes they need to make to fulfill orders, the ones that need to go to the oven, as well as wondering if any orders will be missing and if the dough will be enough.

There is a permanent concern whether the cardboard boxes collected by Fernando Gentil in the supermarkets will be sufficient to accommodate all the breads and cookies to be distributed. Cardboard boxes could be a huge cost to the cooperative if they needed to be purchased. Bianca comments that neither Modelo nor Sol e Mar return the boxes in which the products are delivered:

> Some are offered, but if it's over, we must buy. We can't send the cookies in the bags and each box was 1 Euro and a half plus VAT. Each cake costs 2.50 and a box takes six cakes and goes and stays, doesn't come back. There are weeks when they take five or six boxes and keep them.

Carolina asks, in a moment of the night, if I will remember them or miss her when I go to Brazil. I say yes, I will miss them all a lot. I notice a certain emotion in Carolina's eyes and voice, and I also get emotional. I tell her that when we live with someone out of obligation, I do not necessarily miss the person, but that when it is because we want to, by our choice, in these cases we miss them. I repeat that I am learning a lot from them and enjoying being there.

Bianca's husband, Fernando, arrives around 6.30 am to take two boxes of cookies to Modelo. After a while, he finds out that I have never ate rabbit and invites me to have lunch at his house on Sunday. I reply that I will be a little embarrassed, shy, but he insists. Before I leave, Bianca explains how to get to her home.

Megasil finds it extremely difficult to obtain funds for extraordinary activities, such as equipment failures, infrastructure investments, among others. Precisely for cases like these, Andrea talked to a friend of hers, who said that the state's recognition of Megasil as IPSS equivalent would only bring advantages to the organization. However, Andrea's greatest fear is about the loss of autonomy concerning the cooperative's management:

> Because we stop being owners... in a way... because the IPSS, I think it turns out to be an institution that the Government can give us... so... we haven't settled yet how it is... I still don't know how IPSS works, but the cooperative is in charge... it's our control, right? We apply for a subsidy for this, I don't know what... or the Chamber or the Government, but that is ours, right? We are the owners. And the IPSS... the government is in a way the boss... I think that's how it works. That is ours... if you want to do it, we do it, if you don't want to, we don't do it... the consequences are for us.

Bianca, optimistic as always, suggests that they should try this alternative: *"when we have something, we don't waste time... whenever we have an opportunity"*. She says that she even talked to Carlos Bastos about the desire and that he indicated that they should request it in writing.

The girls say they have made a request - sent by letter about two months ago - for the IAS about IPSS status. However, they still have not received any response: *"We are waiting for an answer, waiting them to arrange a meeting with us. We know that when it comes to the Government, even the little things always take time"*.

I realize that there is no full knowledge about what the IPSS status can provide to Megasil, as well as about the procedures for this issue:

> they say that we will be exempt from VAT, that we can make an annual report with our needs for the following year, to ask the Government, and that it will be approved, with transportation needs, for salaries, for works, and the government gives. I don't know, we haven't studied yet to see how IPSS work.

It is also possible to feel the government's disregard for their work, in addition to a strong sense of belonging to the institution and great pride in being the owners of their enterprise, in being able to manage their work. All make it clear that they do not want to be dependent on the government and that they want to continue to own their destinies within the organization, as I mentioned earlier.

Carolina once again recalls that Letícia Moura knew about the possibility that Megasil could receive IPSS status and that she never mentioned it to them, she did not even give the idea. Andrea reflects that, in practice, Megasil has worked as an IPSS for a long time:

> we were already working as an IPSS, we just didn't receive it, we just aren't recognized. We do not pay, but we give work to the girls who come from the Minimum Income. We already are, but we don't have a name, because we already integrate staff... For years... we have been doing this for years.

I suggest that, if they have already sent the letter to IAS, and if they want, the first thing we can do is schedule an appointment with Carlos Bastos or bring him to the cooperative. Bianca replies that it would be good if he were to visit Megasil's facilities, as he could see how they work.

I get in touch with Carlos Bastos and settle an appointment for Friday, May 22, which was canceled by the unavailability of Carlos' agenda. I try again to schedule a meeting, but the second date is also cleared. In the third attempt, on June 5, 2009, the meeting finally takes place. I spend the night working at Megasil from 4 to 5 June until 1:30 am, before going home to get some sleep. At 10:50 am I pick up Carlos Bastos directly at the IAS to take him to Megasil, in Lagoa.

Even after the dawn of work we meet Bianca and Andrea. Lucia, Emanuela, and the girl who is cleaning today have arrived for normal hours. As soon as we enter, Andrea takes Carlos to get to know the cooperative's facilities. I see, on the bench where the Portuguese sweet bread is wrapped in plastic wrap, pieces of dough in the shape of a leg, head, and a doll, carefully decorated with beans representing his eyes. Bianca had explained to me that these pieces are used for religious promises.

The conversation between Carlos Bastos and Andrea begins with the question regarding the possibility of Megasil application for IPSS status. Carlos comments that IAS has only received a letter from Megasil, which Andrea shows the copy. He says that in this letter, only Megasil's intention was expressed, but he pledges to e-mail the list of necessary documents and says that the sooner the co-op sends this documentation, the sooner he will forward the process for analysis by IAS legal department.

Andrea says she thinks she has already sent, along with the letter, some of the documents that Carlos mentioned verbally, such as a copy of the cooperative's bylaws. Carlos shows an expression of doubt, of ignorance on the subject, and then says that if they have already sent, they do not need to send again, but only those who have not yet been sent.

In some cases, some adjustments and/or corrections are required in the cooperatives' statutes, but Carlos hopes that it is not Megasil's case, considering that it would imply spending more time and financial resources with a notary.

Carlos visits the cooperative's office and talks about the issue of computers and systems, always talking about the possibilities of government aids after positive recognition as IPSS. He also talks about the possibility of paying a 'coordinator' for the cooperative, a person to take specific care of management issues, stressing the importance of having someone to 'think' about management, being able to dedicate time to it. Carlos says that expenses with cleaning supplies and accounting services can also be requested, which would eventually 'release' a part of the current expenses so that wages would increase.

He also emphasizes the importance of a thorough attention to the expenditure of received funds, since when a value is destined for a certain purpose, it cannot be spent on something else, and must be returned in case of non-use and case of partial use. Andrea says that this is a question of planning and organization, but Carlos says that many organizations are unable to comply with this type of accountability.

Carlos talks about Cresaçor and the CORES brand. The girls listen in silence. Carlos replies that the employee of the legal department who takes care of the IPSS status is on vacation and should return only on the 9th, but believes that if they send the documents soon, by the end of June they should receive some kind of response about their application.

Carlos tastes the dough and talks about his brother and grandmother. In a relaxed mood, he does not even use the napkins that Bianca had quickly provided. At the end of the visit, Bianca gives Carlos three bags of biscuits, just as she did with us when we started to go there always.

Carlos thanks us for 'providing this visit to him' and confesses that there had been more than two years since he last visited any organization, and that he liked the experience a lot. He puts himself available once again at the IAS.

Until the visit, even with the receipt of the letter, IAS never did anything to attend Megasil, did not even reply to the letter sent, contacted by phone, made a visit through a technician, or sent a list of documents.

Another point that deserves to be mentioned is the payment of someone to take care of the cooperative's management, considering that this could pose a risk to the co-op's values, with someone coming from outside and 'hired to do that'.

Carlos's positioning shows the IAS vision and this is even more explicit when he says that they need someone to only think about the management of the cooperative, showing a clear separation between managing and doing, in addition to calling into question the capacity of the members to run an organization of their own.

It is interesting to note how Carlos speaks of the importance of visiting these organizations, of these institutions different characteristics, but the 'mapping' about SE designed by Ronaldo Rosa Amparo, conducted by IAS and led by Jaime Marins was not carried out based on this view.

In another moment at Megasil, talking to Bianca, Andrea, and Carolina about Carlos's visit, I ask about the issue of Cresaçor, which Carlos had already talked about during the visit. Bianca and Andrea comment that they have not heard of it and that they have no idea how it works. Carolina says that she knows Cresaçor and has been there, showing a good understanding of the organization's functionality:

> I know what Cresaçor is because I already had it there. if you go to Cresaçor, they have their tendencies. This Cresaçor does not help everyone. I already went to this Cresaçor and we were not helped either. I've been to meetings there. That is a mother cooperative.

Marina Bianca asks: "*do we need to be affiliated with Cresaçor to receive the IPSS status?*". I reply that one thing is separate from the other, at least theoretically. The Azorean Government's version of the 'Solidarity Economy' confuses Megasil members.

Bianca is optimistic all the time: "*I am hopeful that now it will be [IPSS]... they are interested... and his talk [Carlos Bastos] here, the advice he gave, as we should do... I think so*". While she dreams, makes plans, and thinks about strategies to achieve them, Andrea and Carolina are more 'down-to-earth', warning her that they first need to wait to know if the request will be approved by the IAS.

When we ask if Megasil members have heard of Solidarity Economy, silence takes over the room. Nobody knows the concept. Bianca and Andrea are now talking about the future of Megasil. Andrea says that better working conditions are needed. Bianca talks again about the meaning of work, which goes beyond making money:

> it costs me to see... I fought so hard for 22 years... even though I won little, I always fought... and so now there are new people to catch... but I would like them to come here to work it wasn't just to earn your money at the end of the month... to work here to get a job, to have a salary... the person should be here because the person likes it.

On August 6, 2009, I arrive at Megasil, and Bianca is there again with her youngest daughter, Greta. Everyone had already commented that she is very interested in learning about the organization and its work. I ask Greta if she went there due to pressure or her will and she promptly replies that it was her will. Bianca explains that she had an event to go to but preferred to work at the cooperative. The girl says that today she will stay awake: "*today I am not going to sleep*" and work all night, since the next day she started working with us, but she slept around 2 am with Maria, Lídia's daughter.

When I meet Lídia, Bianca's daughter, in Ponta Delgada, she comments that Bianca is working at Megasil excessively, beyond her health limits. She comments that for herself, Lídia, she would not be able to reconcile her current job at Azores Store with her job at Megasil, having a private life and taking care of her children.

Bianca says she wanted them to have a table with more comfortable chairs for them to rest at least 20 minutes at lunchtime, as well as a microwave oven to heat the food. And today, what would be your greatest wish here in the cooperative? Your greatest need, dream, I ask.

> The biggest need is the money. And for the rest... I don't know... more staff to work with, but that we could pay... because we have two there, and now we will have another deaf girl dumb from social assistance... but it is a job thing until noon... because if we could pay them anything else, they would come all day... and right now the workforce is lacking.

I comment on the need to go to Brazil for family health issues and sadly say goodbye with 'see you soon, Megasil!'. I am touched and I comment with them that it is because Megasil is not just work, it is not just making cookies and selling. Bianca complete:

> No... it's much more than that ... if we go to work in a factory... a factory that has existed for years... it is one more employee who goes there... but no... that it was born in my hands, it started with a bread I brought from home... a bowl... which I will show you what it is because I don't know if you know what it is... so it started with dishes I brought home, a wooden spoon. We brought a lot of things from home to get started. This was born in my hands, that's why I like it a lot... I like it a lot... and I feel sorry for a day that I can't work because I'm not eternal... or fall or be like that with people who don't know how to take it forward as I have so far... it will hurt me a lot... it will hurt me a lot because then for me it has a lot of sentimental value because it's not just my job... and that's it... In a factory, somewhere, it's not the same as I have here.

Megasil in 2010

July 8, 2010. In a hypermarket on São Miguel island, I look at the packaged and labeled cookies waiting for whoever takes them home. My first action is to find out if they are fresh when they were manufactured and their expiration date. I look around and notice that the Portuguese sweet bread is also available, wrapped in a plastic wrap. The closed plastic packaging holds more than just delights for the palate.

How many drops of sweat are needed so the customers can enjoy moments of gastronomic delight? How are the Portuguese sweet breads made? How are the people who produce these delights? What time do you work to make that dough so fresh? Do they receive fair wages? The dimension of everything that, together, needs to be orchestrated for the products to be ready and fresh on the market shelf is not within reach.

I leave the market and go to Lagoa, about ten kilometers from Ponta Delgada. The bus leaves Ponta Delgada and takes about twenty-five minutes on the trip. I arrive at the cooperative doors at ten to nine, on this Thursday night in the Azorean summer. It is July, but it is not as hot as in Lisbon and, with a temperature that may be around twenty-three degrees Celsius. The thermal sensation is mild.

Another night of work begins at Megasil, with the day still clear. As I approach the cooperative's windows, I already see Bianca focused on the electric dough mixer. 10 pm and the flour will produce small and large breads: "*Now we produce dough also from Monday to Tuesday. We used to produce 110 kilos. Today we have already made 160, double the mass, twice a week. We're doing twice as much as when you were here*".

Bianca explains that this production increase regarding the Portuguese sweet bread started during Easter of 2010, due to the acquisition of this product by Modelo hypermarket, which until then only used to buy Megasil's cookies: "*They called here to say that they liked our bread, saying that they had customers who asked for 'dough from Lagoa' and they didn't have it*".

In the contract regarding the supply of Portuguese sweet bread for Modelo, Bianca included a clause explaining that she accepts returns of unsold products only in the event of a mistake made by Megasil, such as if they were delivered without the expiration date labels. She says, with some indignation, that this hypermarket takes up to ninety days to pay them.

The new contract resulted in a necessary increase in Megasil's production of Portuguese sweet bread. Only today, approximately four hundred will be produced, between small and large. In terms of comparison, that number was around two hundred last year. This increase in the production of Portuguese sweet bread in a cooperative that was already struggling to meet its previous production does not happen without consequences. Bianca says that she has been trying to stock biscuits for months, but she cannot, producing only what is necessary to serve open orders, which ends up preventing Megasil from even entering other markets and stores with its products:

> I don't know if you know... there are several stores in various parts of the island... they have been waiting for us for three months... for cookies ... how will we put a cookie if we don't have the capacity? They compete with Modelo and Sol e Mar... I have their director's contact in my portfolio... I wanted to make a small inventory for a long time... but I can't.

Bianca explains that, since the aforementioned increase in production, they also started to work in the mornings from Monday to Tuesday (from three to nine in the morning), in addition to still 'turning' from 9 pm on Thursday to 9 am on Friday. The number of Megasil workers in the early hours has surprisingly decreased. Today there are only four people: Bianca, Andrea, Carolina, and Greta (not Bianca's daughter, but an adult of the same name). Greta is a new worker who is twenty years old and who, for the time being, works with them only on Tuesdays and Fridays.

Carolina is not there. Bianca explains that she can no longer spend all nights with her due to the need to assist her mother, 83, who needs care. Carolina now arrives at three in the morning, and together with Greta, the new member, stay until approximately 9 am. In turn, Bianca and Andrea arrive at nine in the evening and stay until three or four in the morning.

Bianca also comments that Lúcia has only arrived around noon to work with the cookies and that, since today she is the only one, she receives from RMG and not directly through Megasil, they cannot charge her that much. To make matters worse, Emanuela has been on medical leave for several months since she had a surgery and should only return in August 2010. Nesia, Andrea's sister-in-law, is in line to operate her other fist (she had already operated one in the first half of 2009), and absent from daily work at the cooperative, against her own will. Andrea, therefore, has always gone in the evenings and late nights.

The cooperative, therefore, has new opening hours: from Monday to Tuesday the activities start at three in the morning. In the early hours of Thursday to Friday, there are two shifts, one from nine to three and another from three to nine in the morning on Friday.

I comment that I am shocked by the current amount of work, with even fewer people working. Bianca says that they divided the dawns into two shifts due to the increase in orders and the fact that she no longer works overnights every day.

Sweat, love, tiredness, and sleep are also constantly present ingredients. Bianca and Andrea did not spend the day resting to dedicate this morning to work. Quite the opposite. Andrea has already devoted a good part of her day taking care of her teenage children, her husband, the house, in addition to having worked almost full time in her grocery store. Bianca has also had to take care of her husband, daughters, and grandchildren, in addition to having already worked during the day at Megasil (usually from nine in the morning to three in the afternoon).

Andrea says she doesn't know anyone who suffers what Bianca suffers during Megasil's daily life and that she is there because she likes it, making it clear that Megasil is not just about work: *"it's like family. Personal situations happen and we try to resolve them. Here we behave like father, mother, aunt, grandmother, brother. This is an institution of social solidarity. We don't have the money, but we have the name"*, she adds, laughing.

From the electric mixer, after more than an hour of operation, almost six pots (large plastic bowls) are filled, which yield approximately sixty large Portuguese sweet bread (one kilo each).

In the pans, the dough that has been mixed for more than an hour is now divided and has its deserved rest. Covered by cloth towels, they now rest for about an hour, before being manually divided into the weight of each cake, passed in the flour, weighed, arranged again in the hands, and individually placed in greased forms. After another rest of almost an hour, they are all painted with eggs and finally go to the oven. The masses rest, but Bianca and Andrea do not.

It is interesting to note that it is practically impossible for a person to carry one of the pans alone, due to the dough's great weight. I try to do this adventure, but I am warned by Bianca that I will not be able to stand alone, which is confirmed right from the start. Thankfully, I am counting on her.

The dishes rest, where there is room for them, in the tight quarters of Megasil's kitchen and, to take them to the tables where the aluminum molds await the dough. Bianca and Andrea help each other and carry them around, transporting them to a wooden chair placed right next to these tables. The intention is that, with the pots next to the table on which the shapes are, and with the scale also at the side, at a slightly less uncomfortable height, they will be able to minimize at least part of the repetitive and tiring effort of this stage of the productive process.

Approximately sixty large breads come out, which means that for each of them, Bianca needs to bend down towards the cake resting on the chair, cut the dough with her hands greased with lard, lift the trunk again, flour part of this dough in a flour recipient next to the pan, weigh the cut dough on the scale placed on a lard pot also supported on the same chair and check if it is necessary to take a little or add more dough so that the weight is right. Only after these procedures she delivers the future bread to Andrea, responsible for carefully and quickly 'folding' it, turning it over and placing it in the previously greased aluminum form. All these muscular, bony, energetic efforts are carried out by these women, at dawn like today, more than four hundred times, and they are not the only ones.

It is impossible not to notice the sweat that runs down Bianca, Andrea's face, and my face. Bianca had already warned me to wear short pants since the nights have been hot. Following their advice, I help them by taking the freshly baked breads to cool down on a metal shelf covered with empty flour bags. After forty minutes, each is unmolded, wrapped in plastic wrap, weighed, labeled, and boxed.

Curious, I ask what gives more financial return to the cooperative, that is, which product yields more, among the biscuits, homemade bread, and Portuguese sweet bread. Neither Bianca nor Andrea knows how to answer me, but the second comments: *"we never critically analyzed our prices because there is a lot of free labor, schedules that you don't pay"*.

I ask if they know for how much their bread is being sold at Modelo. Andrea laughs: for three Euros. Bianca is thoughtful. I say that the large one is sold for 3.29 Euros and Bianca, still thoughtful, goes: *"markets are the ones who win everything, as they still discount what they pay us a percentage for the promotion, for the card, so I don't know any more what"*. Andrea confirms that, after all the discounts, they receive approximately only 2.10 Euros for each big bread.

The records and administrative follow-up at Megasil, as already admitted in 2009 by Andrea and Bianca, are rarely performed and many of the things are kept only in the memory of their members. It is no exaggeration to say that the organization does not function in administrative terms if Bianca and Andrea are not present. And they remain fully aware of this: *"we needed a person [to do] what Andrea does. Doing things in the office, checking in the merchandise. We have things to fill every day and there is no time"*.

During a work night, I sit with them to estimate the costs of their produced products. They comment that there are so many people there on the island who do not help them and that I went from Brazil. I reply that I am not doing any favor, it is their merit and hard work.

We had great difficulty in calculating the production volumes for 2009 and 2010 due to the scarcity of records, but we managed to arrive at approximate numbers so that, finally, we could get an idea of the raw material costs for a large one-kilo bread: 0.666 Euro.

At all times, Bianca is curious and eager to know *"if this is doing something or not, otherwise, I better be at home sitting in my chair"*, she says jokingly. Then he adds: *"I have a lot of love for this here, this is not just a financial issue for me"*, says Bianca.

The cardboard boxes used for transportation remain a constant source of anxiety and concern. They are expensive to be purchased: each box costs around 1.50 Euro and takes only five big cakes and five small ones. Usually, Fernando Gentil, Bianca's husband, and distributor of Megasil's products, goes to the markets to collect empty cardboard boxes on the days they are available. Week after week, Megasil's members are concerned about whether the available boxes will be enough for that week's orders.

Another interesting thing that aroused when elaborating the products' cost structure was that if Megasil had to buy all the cardboard boxes it uses, 11,200 Euros per year would be necessary just for this purpose.

Megasil could benefit a lot from planning in several ways: greater clarity regarding what they spend, what they earn, how much they are working, and, mainly, what they need to continue in this endeavor, with health and solidarity, for at least, other 22 years.

It is after 1 am and the heat and sweat are consuming me. In Megasil's facilities, there are windows with anti-insect screens, but still, the thermal sensation is hot, since there is no air conditioning and two ovens are connected simultaneously, adding to this the heavy and intense work rhythm. Sweat is a constant companion.

I open one of the cooperative's doors and leave to get some air on the street. Even though it is a summer night, there is a gentle wind that seems cold when it slides over the beads of sweat on my skin. Two minutes looking at the stars and getting some fresh air are enough for me to restore some of my energy. Back at work, I hear some news and stories that happened in those eleven months when I stayed physically away from Megasil and its members. Many of these stories, unpublishable, carry with them a certain amount of confessions and, consequently, of great trust shared between us.

The clock is approaching half-past one in the morning and the four hundred pieces of bread must be ready by Friday morning. From going up and down the steps, carrying weight, and spending so many hours standing without breaks, the two minutes of the fresh air outside are no longer effective.

My sore feet are showing another sign of tiredness, even though, like them, I am wearing sneakers. Andrea sits on the steps and almost closes her eyes. We joke that sleep is coming. Bianca is, since the beginning, in full swing. I sit on a stool in the kitchen, next to the electric oven and the sink. My feet breathe easily, and I immediately look at Bianca: her feet are quite swollen, and the swelling already extends to the ankle and the beginning of the shin, showing the merciless consequences of the countless dawns dedicated to Megasil.

As the night goes on Bianca and Andrea's desire and concern to leave work as early as possible for Carolina and Greta increases. But there comes a time when the work begins not to yield as much as they would like to. As we weigh the dough on the scale, I warn Andrea that she is almost making some mistakes due to her inattention and tiredness. She admits that after a certain time she can no longer perform the same way.

It is two o'clock in the morning and Andrea is showing signs of tiredness and sleep. I feel a mixture of tiredness, heat, and sleep. She sits down again, now for about five minutes. Andrea prepares breakfast in the kitchen while Bianca keeps an eye on the ovens. When Andrea comes back with three cups, we sit down and drink coffee - mine pure, Andrea's with sweetener and Bianca's with milk - along with a freshly baked dough: a delight in every way.

I take the time off - the first of the night after five hours of uninterrupted work - to comment with them about the heavy workload for a small group today. Bianca says it has been a big challenge for them and Andrea comments that she has faced "one day at a time". Bianca adds that she likes what she does and repeats it with great emphasis.

How far will Bianca's health allow this pace of work? She always says that, if she can, she will bake until she is a hundred years old and that she considers herself a very agitated person to stay at home idle, which would be her end.

Andrea comments that Megasil has already received a letter from the IAS with the approved IPSS status. However, she warns that the letter only informed this and that neither she nor Bianca knows what the next steps are:

> we received since March, in terms of the pension discount, we had 3% discounts: we paid 30% and now we pay 27%. But we wanted to know the rest as it is. IPSS status is okay, but what about subsidies? I called them to meet Suzana Simões, a lawyer, but I call... and she's

> busy... she won't call back... I call again, she's busy training and does not return... if you must buy equipment, if you need this or that, I did it for that year... we only have one statement, but what good is a statement? How can I do what I need to do if I can't pay? We have been dragging ourselves for 20 years... only now that they recognized, then they should do it right, right?

If, on the one hand, it is interesting to know that Megasil has already received the positive letter from the IAS since March, on the other hand, it is frustrating to know that up to the present moment they enjoy only a discount of approximately 3% in the installments paid to Social Security.

Carlos Bastos suggests that the first thing Megasil can do is take the agency's director to the cooperative *"so that she can feel, smell, see, hear Megasil"*, since there is still no individual agreement established between IAS and the cooperative.

The budget for the acquisition of cardboard boxes, for example, can be requested from IAS, but first, a bilateral agreement must be established. It is worth remembering that, according to Bianca and Andrea, they have been trying to arrange a meeting to discuss this agreement since they received the letter, without success.

Once again, the relationship seems very distant, and communication is even more difficult: the public administration seems to have little interest in assisting the public, which should be its reason for existing.

It is not possible to see profit as a maxim at Megasil, much less its dominant contemporary version of 'profit at any price'. In the cooperative, there is a concern with low earnings and a clear will to increase them. However, attention is primarily dedicated to the means used to carry out the work they do, to how daily life is organized and developed.

The attitude towards other organizations that manufacture similar products is an excellent example to portray some of the values practiced in/by Megasil. They do not want to conquer more market if this implies the risk that other people, organized in other associations and cooperatives, will have no income. They do not want to conquer the market, implying the loss of other people's survival conditions.

As already mentioned, it is then impossible to separate work and income from love, mutual care, trust, professional training, and friendship.

Throughout collective experiences, the relationship with Megasil members grew closer. I remember as if it were today when Andrea looked at me with suspicious eyes at her market. Later, we remember that moment together and ask her how she felt. Her response speaks about how trust builds relationships for her: "*I prepare myself. I let you talk. As I speak, I slowly prepare to know what I'm going to answer... it may be the police, it may be the judiciary, it may be everything*", she says, laughing about arriving at her grocery store.

I also remember that when I first arrived at Megasil, Bianca was very serious. After so many months together, she shows another mood, always playing with me. On the first visit, Emanuela and Lúcia barely looked in my direction and, much less, addressed me. As of May 21, 2009, Bianca and Carolina not only receive me but also dress me in an apron and include me in their work and socializing routines at Megasil.

I am increasingly welcomed by everyone at Megasil. Lúcia is already expressing herself much more. Emanuela welcomes me with kisses and warm hugs.

Bianca asks why I chose Megasil. I recount once again the trajectory that took me to the cooperative, emphasizing the importance of living and feeling an example of an organization that was structured after collective mobilization and not 'top-down' or by government initiative. Carolina says:

> I liked it very much... if it were someone else, you would not be interested, and the funniest thing is that you wanted to find a cooperative that was not in the government... you know? I wanted to know if there were any that were not covered in that, right? This is the most interesting for us... you were interested in what was out.

At a certain point in the morning, while we are packing cookies, Bianca and Carolina notice the way I fill the transparent bags and start to laugh. I ask why they are laughing, and they explain that I put the cookies in the bag stacked in two parallel rows, while they fill the bags at random. I then ask if I am doing it wrong and they say no, that just as I said I learn a lot from them, that they also learn from me, seeming to have liked the way I arranged the cookies.

Weeks later, as we bag cookies during another dawn of working together, I notice that people are now bagging cookies in rows, just as I did. Bianca says: "*someone taught... someone taught*". Surprised, I question if they liked the idea and Carolina comments: "*it looks better... it looks different... it looks better*". And, besides, "*it is better when packing the bags with cookies in the cardboard boxes, breaking fewer cookies during transportation*". Bianca comments that she thought it was a good idea and that they intend to continue. Andrea, with her commercial skills, says that for the customer this visual presentation is important, because he sees that the cookies are not broken. Bianca already has a 'clinical eye' for news and for realizing potential changes that can bring improvements: she leverages inventions and takes risks.

I am surprised to see how every detail, every attitude, no matter how small, relaxed, and unnoticed, is carefully watched by them. More than that, it surprised me how they are, especially Bianca, open to the new, trying to do things in other ways, even when it was something I did not even suggest or think about that possibility.

Bianca says that if I stay in São Miguel, she invites me to become a Megasil member. I hug her, thank her, laughing, and I say that therefore I am shy: *"it's a way to get comfortable with your shyness"*, she replies, laughing too.

I was physically away from Megasil for almost a year, but I am overcome by the feeling that it seems that I was there last month, that time has stopped, that we have not been away that long. I tell Bianca, Carolina, and Andrea that I am very happy to be at the cooperative once again and they reply: *"it seems that you never left here, did you?"*.

Many hours together. Many late nights working together. Conversations, confessions, and discussions on the most diverse subjects. Since May 2009, when I first got in touch with Andrea at her grocery store, I feel that I became, at least a little, part of a different, reinvented Megasil. And that, since then, Megasil has also become part of me, who am not the same either.

CONSIDERATIONS

In a work with cartographic inspirations, as I have emphasized since the beginning of this book, generalizations and the assertion of definite truths are not sought. All knowledge refers to experiences and is circumstantial.

It is not my goal to demonstrate the veracity of propositions and/or hypotheses, but rather to do science by living, experiencing, learning together, listening to others, paying attention to the marks of the encounters, the feelings and instabilities that cross the coexistence, that is, the affections. So, how would it be possible to summarize experiences?

The intention of this section is not to summarize the 'findings' of the research, considering that according to the cartographic method, no data is found or collected: the research is lived and built collectively among all those involved.

I am an integral part of the investigation and I witness my own movements to know what was not waiting for me, but which is built between me and all the other participants. It is not an exaggeration to repeat that the analyzes happen throughout the experiences and not in a separate moment, a posteriori.

I also consider it important to emphasize that I try not to conclude by the people involved since there is no single meaning for the experiences experienced. What I present is the result of how I was affected in each space-time: a cartography of circumstances.

According to the objectives explained in the introduction of this work, I dedicate this section to add some considerations, mainly in the form of questions related to what the cartographics point out about Solidarity Economy.

Management and Solidarity Economy

Undoubtedly, an important point when analyzing Solidarity Economy organizations is how their management is carried out. SE initiatives face challenges to their consolidation, especially as they seek values that go head-to-head with the capitalist logic. However, in most of them, difficulties concerning their management are perceived so that they don't get far from their basic values and allow its members to survive with dignity.

It is not an easy task to think about self-management and ways to manage organizations where profit is not above everything else and that do not push them from their values and objectives, especially when they are inserted in environments where most of the stimuli go towards individualism, and wild competition.

Gabriel Kraychete comments that members of SE, in general, "do not have the adequate knowledge to the economic and associative viability of the activities they carry out"[1]. Often, when starting an associative organization, workers have little information about what this new institutional regime represents, since 67% of those interviewed by Pinto[2], said they have no idea what a 'self-management company' is.

But what do I mean when I talk about management? I refer to a human issue present in any experience, where it is necessary to make something work without fixing itself to standardized forms, which quickly become obsolete[3].

Inspired by Kátia Aguiar[4], rather than addressing the problem of management, I reflect on a "way of putting management as a problem". The modes of management, generated in the social field and disseminated in everyday life (including work), refer to how humans produce their activities and invent ways of being.

More than a central theme, "management seems to have become the

1   KRAYCHETE, G. Economia popular solidária: sustentabilidade e transformação social. 2006. Available at: http://www.capina.org.br. Accessed on: 10 mar 2010, p. 2.

2   PINTO, J. R. L., op. cit., p. 140.

3   SCHWARTZ, Y. Le paradigme ergologique ou um métier de philosophe. Toulouse: Octanès Editions, 2000.

4   AGUIAR, K. Economia dos setores populares: modos de gestão e estratégias de formação. Dez 2006. Available at: www.capina.org.br. Accessed on: 10 may 2010, p. 4.

remedy for any evil or condition for the success of any initiative"[5], largely because the modes of management and production are productions of worlds, of existence.

It is not simple to create and carry out the invention of other ways of working in the contemporary world since survival is imperative and never easy. This need for survival can often expand and realize creative potential. However, these possibilities can also be understood as the effects of poverty and social inequality.

One of the pillars of capitalist subjectivity policies is a corporate conception of management based on prescriptive techniques and procedures, preferably treated as apolitical and neutral. It captures and disqualifies knowledge accumulated in the daily practical activities of the population in favor of a concept of efficiency that is synonymous with greater productivity and profit, with minimal financial costs.

The resulting social and environmental costs are not computed there, as well as their relationship with the limited number of beneficiaries[6]. In other words, the ends and results matter more than the means employed to achieve them. And that, unfortunately, seems to expand and become natural for all dimensions of life.

According to these policies, profit maximization represents the greatest benefit to be achieved and the minimum cost is achieved by reducing the number of jobs and wages paid, converting common and natural goods into raw materials, naturalizing and expanding of capitalist values as human, among others.

In 1911, Frederick Taylor, considered by many as one of the main precursors of contemporary management as a science, already made clear the direction of his wishes and goals when he stated:

> cooperative experiments have failed, and, I think, are generally destined to fail, for several reasons, among which the first and most important, is that no form of cooperation has been developed to date in which each individual is allowed free space for their ambition folks. Personal ambition has always been and will continue to be a more powerful incentive than a desire for general well-being[7].

Management is treated and disseminated as a science, mostly based on standardization, and anchored in almost ideal situations. It produces

5   AGUIAR, K., op. cit., p. 5.

6   PINTO, J. R. L., op. cit., p. 76.

7   TAYLOR, F. W. Shop Management. New York: Harper & Brothers, 1911.

subjectivities shaped according to the interests of capitalist logic.

Meanwhile, the self-managing dimension can add improvisation to the operating modes prescribed by the rules, favoring the invention and production of other subjectivities. It is because of this possibility that the way work is organized must be questioned and questioned[8].

Understanding what management is on the part of SE organizations and their members is very important and must be considered. When it comes to the internal organization of work[9], it is common to see different understandings of management in the same collective. This variation can be (and often is) identified by some people as a difficulty or deficiency in the formation of group members when the criteria used for such an analysis are centered on the corporate capitalist logic, based on the naturalization of organizational values and their homogenization by all its members.

Instead, it is possible to understand these different conceptions and ways of managing in a group as part of the multiplicity that constitutes it. In this case, it is necessary to bear in mind that each member has different ways of acting, feeling, thinking, being, and, consequently, managing. It is by respecting the multiplicity and differences that the invention of the new can be exercised and enhanced.

It is not a matter of seeking to discover and apply the best model and/or management model, but of collectively reflecting on the work developed together, on the values shared by the group and on the conditions in which the work takes place. What does each person think? What does each individual want? How can paths be built to meet existing challenges? To what extent do these desires enhance life? What consequences can they bring? What can they raise?

Self-management cannot be separated from life. It is related to a collective construction of modes of working, managing, and living. It goes in the opposite direction to the belief of 'good management', which promotes the idea that there is a right path (or better) and treats workers as mere executors of strategies developed by other people, with different desires and interests.

SE practices and meanings could then impact and even change the perception of efficiency stands for. If this concerns maximum benefit at

---

8   AGUIAR, K., op. cit., p. 7-8.

9   AGUIAR, K., op. cit., p. 4.

the lowest cost, one should ask about the quality of what is a benefit and about the meanings of what is a cost. New behaviors and perceptions about production, work, trade, technique, and consumption may arise from the lived experiences. This would consequently redefine the very terms by which efficiency is understood[10].

Although theoretically there is no boss or manager in SE organizations, many of the projects, policies, statutes, and expert advice - including many professional academics in this category -, even when discussed and accepted by a collective, convey prescriptions[11]. Considering that what is prescribed does not account for the reality of work or the collective needs, these materials need to be used only as a guide, as a reference.

Pinto[12] draws attention to a debate that arises within the SE movement in Brazil regarding the role of the so-called 'advisors' (usually NGOs, unions, or universities), which offer support - including management-related - to SE organizations. He questions to what extent such advisory services may limit the expression of these enterprises' interests, ending up reproducing hierarchical, subordinate, and even dependent relations with these institutions.

This debate needs to be stimulated and extended to also problematize professional academics. Education is necessary to train staff for SE organizations and their support entities[13]. Paul Singer points out that research is also indispensable to understand the reality of SE so that the analysis and evaluation of experiences can be systematized and we can generate proposals that serve to make this other economy more authentic and more effective.

How to train? For what purposes? Who would be able to carry out this type of training? What kinds of training are necessary? In 2005, incubators of SE organizations already existed in thirty-five Brazilian universities and Brazilian government was increasingly considering the participation of

---

10   PINTO, J. R. L., op. cit., p. 75.

11   AGUIAR, K., op. cit., p. 6.

12   PINTO, J. R. L., op. cit., p. 79.

13   SINGER, P. A recente ressurreição da economia solidária no Brasil. In: SANTOS, B. D. S. (Ed.). Produzir para viver: os caminhos da produção não capitalista. Lisboa: Edições Afrontamento, 2003, p. 71-107, p. 103.

these universities as strategic and fundamental for the development of SE[14].

It takes attention and care! Governmental, advisors, and academic goals may not always be in line with those of the thousands of workers in the more than twenty-one associations and cooperatives in SE (only taking into account the classification criteria of the Brazilian government itself). Furthermore, what is the possibility of 'teaching with and for solidarity' when, as Paulo Freire already said[15], "nobody educates anyone, nobody educates themselves, men educate themselves, mediated by the world"?

The management of Solidarity Economy initiatives represents an additional complexity for the consolidation of these organizations. Management as an area of knowledge has traditionally been divided into a public and a private aspect. Founded on different principles and with theoretically different objectives, neither the public nor the private administration seems to be adequate to contribute, without detracting, to the consolidation of initiatives aimed at values such as those of Solidarity Economy.

Even when it comes to the management of education itself, it is not difficult to visualize a real snowball designed to reproduce a vicious cycle: an education based on capitalist assumptions and the administration of education itself based on the same assumptions.

Today managerial theories increasingly serve as a basis for all dimensions of our lives, and, often, the defense of capitalist prescriptions and concepts of efficiency takes place among SE academics and scholars themselves. Supposedly advocating for the sustainability of these ventures, some evaluate SE practices carrying a concept of sustainability and efficiency that is linked to the dominant values, disguised as supposed neutrality or supposed scientific/academic rigor. Some examples are found in the literature produced on the Solidarity Economy and here already cited and referenced.

The importance of looking more often at how things are done should be emphasized, and not just in the name of what is developed, or the results achieved. Raising theoretical flags seems much simpler than

---

14   SINGER, P. A economia solidária vista a partir dos países do sul: Economia solidária no Brasil. In: Actas do Congresso internacional de economia solidária, Ponta Delgada. Centro de Estudos de Economia Solidária do Atlântico, 2005. p. 131-139, p. 136.

15   FREIRE, P. Pedagogia do oprimido. Rio de Janeiro: Paz e Terra, 2002, p. 68.

living them in the daily relationships and endeavors we build.

Therefore, if on the one hand there may seem to be a need to train associate workers to cooperatively manage businesses, on the other hand, this management needs to be aligned with the values and purposes of the associative organizations. The collective construction of what is meant by management, or rather, self-management, is shown to be practical and daily in SE, with at least two concerns:

a) if the objective is that there is a type of self-management that does not push initiatives away from their solidarity values, the knowledge of those involved, of those who actually make Solidary Economy movements and organizations happen, cannot be ignored or neglected;

b) when we look at universities, the programs and courses which are responsible for training managers, as well as their contents, prepare, mostly, professionals oriented towards importing techniques from the 'best' business schools in the world and, therefore, to reproduce capitalist logic.

It is necessary to question our own performance in the field in the different roles we assume, whether as teachers, researchers, friends, and/or companions of these workers. I agree with Luciane Uberti's words when she says that

> it is important to ask for the possibility of new ways of saying true, for the chance to question the evidence ever again, to dispel and retake our problematizations. Who knows, as education workers, we could minimize the eagerness to shape the political will of others, distancing ourselves from the position of preachers of truth and justice[16].

We have to be careful so that the management of collective enterprises and our attitudes in the field do not function as capture devices[17], de-potentiating the objectives of these organizations and/or devaluing their practices and knowledge:

> the production of these resistance strategies encounters countless difficulties that focus mainly on the power of the traditional forms of organization of capitalist work and concern a culture of devaluation and disqualification of the workers' daily and practical knowledge. The device that triggers these forms of disqualification resides, above all, in the belief in the superiority of technical and scientific knowledge and

---

16   UBERTI, L. Estudos pós-estruturalistas: entre aporias e contra-sensos? Educação e Realidade, v. 31, n. 2, p. 95-116, jul/dec 2006, p. 111.

17   DELEUZE, G.; GUATTARI, F. Mil Platôs. Rio de Janeiro: Ed. 34 Letras, 1995.

its disciplinary developments[18].

It seems necessary to reflect and to investigate how individuals perceive and value themselves and their interpersonal relationships, which is commonly avoided[19]. Performance indicators and strategies used by universities and other entities to evaluate SE organizations, including those aimed at qualification and production, cannot be treated as closed packages to be used. Rather, they need to[20] be produced and re-elaborated together, according to these organizations' routines and working modes. These associations and cooperatives usually face diverse and numerous struggles to build their paths and simply do not need ready packages or recipes to act, but to enhance what they try to foster.

Beliefs in the superiority of technical and scientific knowledge seems more clearly noticeable in groups that are still taking their first steps towards self-management after many years of submission to various forms of traditional private corporate hetero-management. In these cases, groups (and the work they do) can function only at the level of task execution, failing to explore the possibilities for inventing products, managing strategies, and creating other ways of working and living.

To think about the creation of other ways of working means[21] to search for the production of dignity and the recognition of the ability of men and women to reflect and produce their ways of living, working, and existing. It is increasingly difficult to disregard that SE requires new references - including theoretical ones - that allow a better understanding of the possibilities that it presents. It is necessary to look at how Solidarity Economy practices "problematize fixed patterns of behavior and forge new bonds and social norms within the scope of economic relations"[22].

It would be naive to idealize SE: the exercise and the realization of its potential can lead to nothing but survival[23], when successful, which would already be a great achievement considering the difficulty that it is to survive

---

18   TITTONI, J., op. cit., p. 14-15.

19   PINTO, J. R. L., op. cit., p. 17.

20   TITTONI, J., op. cit., p. 15-16.

21   TITTONI, J., op. cit., p. 9-10.

22   PINTO, J. R. L., op. cit., p. 62.

23   ROLNIK, S. Despachos no museu: sabe-se lá o que vai acontecer. In: FONSECA, T. M. G.; KIRST, P. G. (Eds.), Cartografias e devires: a construção do presente. Porto Alegre: Editora da UFRGS, 2003, p. 207-218, p. 214.

in the contemporary world for a good part of the seven billion inhabitants of the planet. But I repeat: it is important to think of SE as being defined less "by what is instituted in it and more by what is in it and overflowing"[24]. Probably the greatest highlight in SE initiatives lie[25] on new mental configurations for the ones involved: new subjectivities.

There are efforts to ensure that wealth is distributed more fairly and to create social bonds and senses of belonging to a social group, which has unparalleled relevance in an individualistic world like the current one.

To effectively operationalize other ways of life, it is not enough to offer everyone the opportunity to participate in the game[26]. There must be personal and cultural changes, a break with the spirit of capitalism. Each of us is part of the problem and of the possible solutions, according to the ways we observe, analyze and participate in these experiences.

It is also important to point out that SE initiatives have varying degrees of institutionalization. While in contemporary societies the development of written instruments to safeguard private interests - contracts, agreements, among others - is visible, when observing interpersonal relationships and the various decision-making bodies in these associations and cooperatives, orality is predominant[27] at the expense of drafting 'guarantees' and written documents: most commitments are signed by what is said.

Therefore, showing the importance of face-to-face and oral relationships in this type of organizations[28],[29] is also a task for the 'supporters', whether they are university students or not: we should help in strengthening ties and associative and solidary values, based on equality among all.

It cannot be forgotten that a large part of the thousands of associations and cooperatives has their roots on mobilizations and struggles experienced by their members. These collective experiences can serve, among other things, for the construction and deconstruction of bonds between people,

24   BENEVIDES, R.; PASSOS, E. A instituição e sua borda. In: FONSECA, T. M. G.; KIRST, P. G. (Ed.). Cartografias e devires: a construção do presente. Porto Alegre: Editora da UFRGS, 2003. p. 341-355, p. 344.

25   CAVALCANTE, A. S., op. cit., p. 5.

26   LISBOA, A. D. M., op. cit., p. 112.

27   VALENTIM, I. V. L., op. cit.

28   Idem.

29   PINTO, J. R. L., op. cit.

and solidarity is only true if it is born of voluntary adhesion[30].

Solidarity Economy: for whom?

Different social actors, such as States, NGOs, corporations, universities, and members of social movements, have different conceptions about the Solidarity Economy, including what they consider its objectives, political and economic project. Consequently, they deal with this social phenomenon in different ways.

As a concept created by academics during the 1990s, Solidarity Economy has no consensual definitions. The definitions vary according to the values, worldviews, understandings of the profession itself, and life goals of academic professionals.

One of the contributions of the research I carried out with so many people concerns the lack of research focused on Solidarity Economy specifically in Portugal and also worldwide.

More specifically, in-depth research with members of self-managed organizations in the Autonomous Region of the Azores is needed. And in other countries as well. There is so much we can learn. SE is seen by the Azorean Government as representing a transitional phase between unemployment and the return to a job in private companies. In this conception, concerning the political aspect, these associations and cooperatives are not seen as constructors of organizational forms other than the heterogeneous, now dominant.

The governmental version of the Azorean SE does not pay attention to the values that these organizations build in relationships, the objectives they seek, or the means they use to achieve them.

By the way, it is interesting to note that the Government of the Azores sees as belonging to the Solidary Economy only and exclusively a small group of organizations already known and participating in a single 'mother cooperative', of which academics and a state official are part of the list of founders.

There seems to be no recognition, as belonging to SE, of any other collective organization than those affiliated with Cresaçor. Consequently, those who 'do not enter the game' have their access made difficult to specific Azorean public policies aimed at SE.

In Brazil, in contrast to Portugal, the concept of SE is different for

---

30   LISBOA, A. D. M., op. cit., p. 114.

some academic professionals, but like others. The Brazilian governmental conception resembles the Azorean in some respects, since the National Secretariat for Solidarity Economy was designed and built to create jobs, collective self-employment, for the unemployed, according to an interview given by Paul Singer[31].

Today, in Brazil, there is a bill for this national secretariat to leave the Ministry of Labor and Employment and go to a ministry to be created, dedicated to micro and small companies, which shows a point of approximation between the concepts of the two governments regarding the understanding of these collective organizations.

However, at least in Brazil, several social actors linked to the social phenomenon of Solidarity Economy have built up resistance to this, considering that it would be a mischaracterization of the movement and its values.

Much has been investigated, analyzed, and written about the Solidarity Economy in the last fifteen years, in different areas of knowledge and parts of the world. However, there is still a small number of studies that seek to investigate what SE builds, according to the voices, senses, and feelings of the people who are part of their associations and cooperatives.

We still need to ask: do members of self-management organizations recognize themselves as part of this other economy? Do you know what Solidarity Economy is all about? In your opinion, what does SE label, bring, and enhance these collective endeavors?

Megasil co-op did not initially know the concept of Solidarity Economy. Practices seem to come before conceptualization and people are later adjectives as belonging to this other economy by some, but not always by themselves. The experiences with the members of this organization show that they did not see themselves as belonging to this other economy.

It is a fact that the Solidarity Economy belongs to a field of study for academics, a political flag for some legislators, among other meanings, according to every social actor. For some associations and cooperatives, it may represent a social movement.

But some questions remain: what are the impacts, from the perspective of the people who work in associations and cooperatives, of a concept such as Solidarity Economy? What can the concept bring to the construction of more collaborative, more egalitarian, and fair societies? In the sense that

---

31   SINGER, P. Brasil: El papel del Estado y de la sociedad. America Latina en movimiento, n. 430, p. 20-22, mar 2008.

they achieve their goals. It seems that many times members of organizations considered by some as Solidarity Economy do not even participate in these discussions and, therefore, questions such as those raised in this paragraph can be interesting guiding questions for future investigations.

The experiences I have had with Megasil make me agree with Armando Lisboa when he considers[32] that one of the originalities that some SE organizations bring is that they are on the market without submitting to the pursuit of profit as an ultimate goal. These organizations give up the possibility of maximizing the financial return due to a social perspective that includes, at Megasil, the attitude of considering that all organizations, even competitors, must have space in the market. As Gabriel Kraychete says[33], there is a 'solidarity' that could be understood as irrational for a capitalist company, but that makes sense for the reproduction of life in that organization.

The political character of what is done at Megasil does not seem to be contained only in what its members do - food production - but in the ways they work and live, in what overflows in the relationships they establish, in what they raise and cause in all those establish relations with.

If we consider that Megasil belongs to the so-called Solidarity Economy, is it possible to give exclusive attention to the labor relations that exist in it and to despise the feelings that go through them such as those of friendship and family? Any attempt in this direction may prove to be largely reductive and, above all, disrespectful towards its members and the life project they build.

The way academic professionals see these organizations seems to be of great importance. Therefore, it is worth mentioning that the way these initiatives are seen and the way they are treated and portrayed can serve precisely to block their resistance potential. Two aspects may receive more attention in future research:

a) the necessary humbleness to understand and admit how ignorant we are when we try to build 'true' or 'correct' knowledge about Solidarity Economy based on the rigid principles of contemporary dominant science;

b) investigations that critically analyze the attitudes and the roles of professional academics are needed. It is necessary to put Academia on the spotlight since it demonstrates a great capacity to analyze other

---

32   LISBOA, A. D. M., op. cit., p. 109.

33   KRAYCHETE, G. Economia solidária: conceitos e contexto. Seminário Internacional sobre Economia Solidária: desafios para um novo tempo. Salvador: Fundação Luis Eduardo Magalhães, 2002.

entities, but it still 'crawls' when it comes to analyzing itself.

What is the importance of practicing what we preach? Can Solidarity Economy, as a political project based on other values, be treated as an 'object' of investigation and, in this sense, seek the supposed neutrality and detachment of researchers, without necessarily existing the practice of these values by those who defend scientifically? Can Solidarity Economy be defended without being lived? Can values be preached by people who do not live them? Issues like these can be of great relevance for us to debate a theme like Solidarity Economy today, in societies in which capitalism develops as the dominant logic. Not just as a system of economic production, but as a regime that produces worlds and senses.

If Solidarity Economy is understood and lived as having a political project that seeks values such as solidarity, egalitarianism, and self-management, it seems even more important that these issues are debated so not fall into the trap of, as dazzled by the celebration of our creative force and transgressive and experimental stance, and fascinated by the prestige that comes from it, we voluntarily surrender[34] to pimping[35] promoted by capitalist logic, becoming "the creators of the worlds made for and by capitalism in this new guise"[36].

The values of another economy, as well as other ways of feeling, thinking, and living, can only be consolidated when they exist in the practices of people and groups: new attitudes and sensitivities. The question, therefore, is no longer whether or not we should organize ourselves, but whether or not we are reproducing the dominant modes of subjectification[37] in our daily actions, including those of supposed militancy, criticism, research, and education.

Thinking about Solidarity Economy - if we want to maintain this concept - will require us to make an effort to broaden how we look at people, how

---

34   VALENTIM, I.V.L. Between Academic Pimping and Moral Harassment in Higher Education: an Autoethnography in a Brazilian Public University. Journal of Academic Ethics, v. 16, p. 151–171, 2018. DOI: https://doi.org/10.1007/s10805-018-9300-y.

35   VALENTIM, I.V.L. Academic Pimping. In: Pensoneau-Conway S.L., Adams T.E., Bolen D.M. (eds) Doing Autoethnography. SensePublishers: Rotterdam, 2017. DOI: https://doi.org/10.1007/978-94-6351-158-2_18.

36   ROLNIK, S., op. cit., p. 18.

37   GUATTARI, F.; ROLNIK, S. Micropolítica. cartografias do desejo. Petrópolis: Vozes, 2007, p. 203.

we live with them, as well as what we mean by research and ways of doing it. This, of course, if scientific rigor is understood as, above all, respect for people who build with us what we call science.

End and Beginning

What worlds do we build when we are more and more individualistic? The world is not outside, it is not waiting for us, but we build it with each of our attitudes. We need to believe in the world. Or perhaps to discredit the world we have built to rebuild a more supportive and egalitarian world with each of our daily actions, desires, and feelings.

We need to believe in ourselves and in the other human beings. As Gilles Deleuze says[38], we have completely lost the world, dispossessed of it, and believing in the world mainly means raising events, even small ones, that are out of control, since it is at the level of each attempt that the resistance capacity is evaluated or, on the contrary, submitted to control.

The coexistences that originated this book are inspirations, encouragements, and stimuli for the construction of lives based on other values than those that are dominant today. The values we defend are not just in our minds, just in what we say, but in our attitudes. It seems necessary to believe that we can build new ways of living, feeling, working, acting, and relating. We need to learn how to create these new ways. We must try, dare, face, fight, question. Hope alone is not going to help us if we do not take a step. If we do not act. We need to take a chance!

---

38   DELEUZE, G. Conversações. São Paulo: Ed. 34, 1992, p. 218.

Gorreana Tea
São Miguel Island, Azores
May 16, 2009
Photo by Igor Vinicius Lima Valentim

REFERENCES

AGUIAR, K. Economia dos setores populares: modos de gestão e estratégias de formação. Dec 2006. Available at: www.capina.org.br. Accessed on: 10 mai 2010.

AMARO, R. R. Reflexões sobre a economia solidária. In: Actas do Congresso internacional de economia solidária, 29-30 sep 2005, Ponta Delgada. Centro de estudos de economia solidária do atlântico, 2005, p. 17-29.

AMARO, R. R.; MADELINO, F. Economia Solidária. Contributos para um conceito. 2. ed. Ponta Delgada: Projecto CORES, 2006.

ARRUDA, M. Socioeconomia solidária: desenvolvimento de baixo para cima. Rio de Janeiro: Ed. PACS, 1998.

BAUMAN, Z. Amor líquido: sobre a fragilidade dos laços humanos. Rio de Janeiro: Jorge Zahar Ed., 2004.

BAUMAN, Z. Confiança e medo na cidade. Lisboa: Relógio D'Água Editores, 2006.

BAUMAN, Z. Vida Líquida. Rio de Janeiro: Jorge Zahar Ed., 2007.

BEIERSDORFF, M. B. et al. Educação e trabalho através da Economia Solidária. In: Anais do IV Encontro de Economia Solidária, São Paulo. EDUSP, 2006.

BENEVIDES, R.; PASSOS, E. A instituição e sua borda. In: FONSECA, T. M. G.; KIRST, P. G. (Ed.). Cartografias e devires: a construção do presente. Porto Alegre: Editora da UFRGS, 2003, p. 341-355.

BERTUCCI, A. A.; SILVA, R. M. A. Vinte anos de economia popular solidária: trajetória da Cáritas Brasileira dos PACs à EPS. Brasília: Cáritas Brasileira, 2003.

CARCHEDI, G. The social face of european capitalism. In: TITTENBRUN,

J. (Ed.). Capitalism or Capitalisms? Szczecin: My Book, 2009, p. 44-77.

CARRION, R. M.; VALENTIM, I. V. L.; HELLWIG, B. C. (Orgs.). Residência Solidária UFRGS: vivência de universitários com o desenvolvimento de uma tecnologia social. Porto Alegre: Editora da UFRGS, 2006.

CASTEL, R. As metamorfoses da questão social. Petrópolis: Vozes, 1998.

CHAGAS, W. Mundo e contramundo. Porto Alegre: Editora da UFRGS, 1972.

COCCO, G. Trabalho e cidadania: produção e direitos na era da globalização. 2. ed. São Paulo: Cortez, 2001.

CUNHA, D. Intervenção do secretário regional dos assuntos sociais do governo regional dos Açores. In: Actas do Congresso internacional de Economia Solidária, 29-30 sep 2005, Ponta Delgada. Centro de estudos de economia solidária do atlântico, 2005, p. 13-15.

DELEUZE, G. Conversações. São Paulo: Ed. 34, 1992.

DELEUZE, G. Francis Bacon: la lógica de la sensación. Madrid: Arena Libros, 2002.

DELEUZE, G.; GUATTARI, F. Mil Platôs. Rio de Janeiro: Ed. 34 Letras, 1995.

DESCARTES, R. A discourse of a method for the well guiding of reason, and the discovery of truth in the sciences. London: Printed by Thomas Newcombe, 1649. Available at: http://gateway.proquest.com/openurl?ctx_ver=Z39.88-2003&res_id=xri:eebo&rft_val_fmt=&rft_id=xri:eebo:image:54569. Accessed on: 18 may 2010.

DESCARTES, R. Les principes de la philosophie. In: ADAM, C.; TANNERY, P. (Ed.). Oeuvres de Descartes. Paris: Tomo IX-2, 1971.

ELIAS, N.; SCOTSON, J. L. Os estabelecidos e os outsiders: sociologia das relações de poder a partir de uma pequena comunidade. Rio de Janeiro: Jorge Zahar Ed., 2000.

ENGELMAN, S. Trabalho e loucura: uma biopolítica dos afetos. Porto Alegre: Sulina; Editora da UFRGS, 2006.

FONSECA, T. M. G.; KIRST, P. G. Cartografias e devires: a construção do presente. Porto Alegre: Editora da UFRGS, 2003.

FERREIRA, J. M. C. Portugal no contexto da "transição para o socialismo": história de um equívoco. Blumenau: Editora da FURB, 1997.

FERREIRA, J. M. C. O papel do cooperativismo no desenvolvimento da economia social em Portugal. Verve, n. 2, p. 88-122, oct 2002.

FERREIRA, J. M. C. Da impossibilidade de superar a actual crise do capitalismo. Utopia, n. 26, p. 7-16, jul/dec 2008.

FORRESTER, V. O horror econômico. São Paulo: Editora da Universidade Estadual Paulista, 1997.

FOUCAULT, M. La creación de modos de vidaEstética, ética y hermenéutica. Barcelona: Paidós, 1999.

FOUCAULT, M. Vigiar e punir: nascimento da prisão. Petrópolis: Vozes, 2005.

FRANÇA FILHO, G. C.; LAVILLE, J.-L. A Economia Solidária: uma abordagem internacional. Porto Alegre: Editora da UFRGS, 2004.

FREIRE, P. Pedagogia do oprimido. Rio de Janeiro: Paz e Terra, 2002.

FREIRE, R. A farsa ecológica. Rio de Janeiro: Guanabara Koogan, 1992.

GAIGER, L. I. A economia solidária no Brasil e o sentido das novas formas de produção não capitalistas. CAYAPA - Revista Venezolana de Economía Social, n. 8, p. 9-37, dec 2004.

GALVÃO, A. P. et al. (Eds.) Capitalismo cognitivo: trabalho, redes e inovação. Rio de Janeiro: DP&A, 2003.

GIACOMEL, A. E. et al. Trabalho e contemporaneidade: o trabalho tornado vida. In: FONSECA, T. M. G.; KIRST, P. G. (Ed.). Cartografias e devires: a construção do presente. Porto Alegre: Editora da UFRGS, 2003, p. 137-148.

GOVERNO DOS AÇORES. Empresas e Economia Solidária dão emprego a 210 pessoas nos Açores. Portal do Governo dos Açores. Ponta Delgada, 29 de Setembro de 2005. Available at: http://edt-gra.azores.gov.pt/Portal. Accessed on: 18 out 2008.

GOVERNO DOS AÇORES. Intervenção do presidente do Governo na abertura de uma mesa redonda sobre Pobreza e Exclusão. Portal do Governo dos Açores. Ponta Delgada, 16 de Outubro de 2007. Available at: http://edtgra.azores.gov.pt/Portal. Accessed on: 18 out 2008.

GUATTARI, F. As três ecologias. Campinas: Papirus, 1990.

GUATTARI, F.; ROLNIK, S. Micropolítica: cartografias do desejo. Petrópolis: Vozes, 2007.

GURGEL, C. A gerência do pensamento: gestão contemporânea e consciência neoliberal. São Paulo: Cortez, 2003.

HANDY, C. A era do paradoxo. São Paulo: Makron Books, 1995.

HARDT, M. O trabalho afetivo. In: PELBART, P. P.; COSTA, R. D. (Ed.). O Reencantamento do concreto. Cadernos de Subjetividade. São Paulo: Editora Hucitec, 2003, p. 143-157.

HOVEN, R. v. d. Social work and the third sector in Portugal. Available at: http://cms.euromodule.com/servlet/PB/-s/1xnvo101cbuuyh1kjgtnn9y9cijj lx9g4/show/1027649/po3rd_1.pdf. Accessed on: 10 may 2010. 2003.

KASTRUP, V. O funcionamento da atenção no trabalho do cartógrafo. In: PASSOS, E. et al (Ed.). Pistas do método da cartografia: pesquisa-intervenção e produção de subjetividade. Porto Alegre: Sulina, 2009, p. 32-51.

KIRST, P. G. Redes do olhar. In: FONSECA, T. M. G.; KIRST, P. G. (Ed.). Cartografias e devires: a construção do presente. Porto Alegre: Editora da UFRGS, 2003. p. 43-52.

KIRST, P. G. et al. Conhecimento e cartografia: tempestade de possíveis. In: FONSECA, T. M. G.; KIRST, P. G. (Ed.). Cartografias e devires: a construção do presente. Porto Alegre: Editora da UFRGS, 2003, p. 91-101.

KLEIN, N. The shock doctrine. The rise of disaster capitalism. London: Penguin Books, 2007.

KRAYCHETE, G. Economia solidária: conceitos e contexto. Seminário Internacional sobre Economia Solidária: desafios para um novo tempo. Salvador: Fundação Luis Eduardo Magalhães, 2002.

KRAYCHETE, G. Economia popular solidária: sustentabilidade e transformação social. 2006. Available at: http://www.capina.org.br. Accessed on: 10 mar 2010.

KRISTEVA, J. Sentido e contra-senso da revolta: poderes e limites da psicanálise. Rio de Janeiro: Rocco, 2000.

LAZZARATO, M.; NEGRI, A. Trabalho imaterial: formas de vida e produção da subjetividade. Rio de Janeiro: DP&A, 2001.

LAZZARATO, M. As revoluções do capitalismo. Rio de Janeiro: Civilização Brasileira, 2006.

LEITÃO, C. F. Cartografia de imagens de práticas solidárias. In: Anais do VIII

Congresso Luso-Afro-Brasileiro de Ciências Sociais, Coimbra. Centro de Estudos Sociais, 2004.

LISBOA, A. D. M. Economia Solidária e autogestão: imprecisões e limites. Revista de Administração de Empresas – RAE, v. 45, n. 3, p. 109-115, jul/sep 2005.

MAIRESSE, D. Cartografia: do método à arte de fazer pesquisa. In: FONSECA, T. M. G.; KIRST, P. G. (Ed.). Cartografias e devires: a construção do presente. Porto Alegre: Editora da UFRGS, 2003, p. 259-271.

MATURANA, H. R.; VERDEN-ZÖLLER, G. The origin of humanness in the biology of love. Exeter: Imprint Academic, 2008.

MOTTA, E. D. S. M. A "Outra Economia": um olhar etnográfico sobre a Economia Solidária. (2004). Dissertação de Mestrado (Mestrado em Antropologia Social) - Museu Nacional / PPGAS, Universidade Federal do Rio de Janeiro, Rio de Janeiro, 2004.

NAMORADO, R. A Economia Social - Uma constelação de esperanças. Oficina do CES, n. 213, 2004. Available at: http://www.ces.uc.pt/publicacoes/oficina/213/213.pdf. Accessed on: 27 ago 2005.

NAMORADO, R. Para uma economia solidária - a partir do caso português. Revista Crítica de Ciências Sociais, n. 84, 2009, p. 65-80.

NARDI, H. C. Ética, trabalho e subjetividade: trajetórias de vida no contexto das transformações do capitalismo contemporâneo. Porto Alegre: Editora da UFRGS, 2006.

NEGRI, A.; COCCO, G. GlobAL: biopoder e luta em uma América Latina globalizada. Rio de Janeiro: Record, 2005.

PASSOS, E. et al. Apresentação. In: PASSOS, E. et al (Ed.). Pistas do método da cartografia: pesquisa-intervenção e produção de subjetividade. Porto Alegre: Sulina, 2009, p. 7-16.

PELBART, P. P. Da função política do tédio e da alegria. In: FONSECA, T. M. G.; KIRST, P. G. (Ed.). Cartografias e devires: a construção do presente. Porto Alegre: Editora da UFRGS, 2003, p. 69-78.

PINTO, J. R. L. Economia Solidária: de volta à arte da associação. Porto Alegre: Editora da UFRGS, 2006.

PORTELA, J. A economia ou é solidária ou é fratricida. Revista Crítica de Ciências Sociais, n. 84, p. 115-152, 2009.

REPPOLD, C. R. et al. O trabalho como dispositivo de subjetivação, hierarquia e controle no poder judiciário: um estudo de caso. In: FONSECA, T. M. G.; FRANCISCO, D. J. (Ed.). Formas de ser e habitar a contemporaneidade. Porto Alegre: Editora da UFRGS, 2000, p. 129-136.

ROCHA, M. L. D.; AGUIAR, K. Pesquisa-intervenção e a produção de novas análises. Revista Psicologia Ciência e Profissão, n. 4, p. 64-73, 2003.

ROLNIK, S. Cartografia ou de como pensar com o corpo vibrátil. Núcleo de Estudos e Pesquisas da Subjetividade da PUC/SP, 1987.

ROLNIK, S. A dama de negro. Núcleo de Estudos e Pesquisas da Subjetividade da PUC/SP, 1993.

ROLNIK, S. Pensamento, corpo e devir. Uma perspectiva ético/estético/política no trabalho acadêmico. Cadernos de Subjetividade PUC/SP, v. 1, n. 2, p. 241-251, sep 1993.

ROLNIK, S. Despachos no museu: sabe-se lá o que vai acontecer. In: FONSECA, T. M. G.; KIRST, P. G. (Eds.). Cartografias e devires: a construção do presente. Porto Alegre: Editora da UFRGS, 2003, p. 207-218.

ROLNIK, S. Cartografia sentimental: transformações contemporâneas do desejo. Porto Alegre: Sulina; Editora da UFRGS, 2006.

ROLNIK, S. Com o que você pensa? Núcleo de Estudos da Subjetividade, 2007.

SANTOS, B. D. S. (Ed.). Produzir para viver: os caminhos da produção não capitalista. Lisboa: Edições Afrontamento, 2003.

SANTOS, B. D. S.; RODRÍGUEZ, C. Introdução: para ampliar o cânone da produção. In: SANTOS, B. D. S. (Ed.). Produzir para viver: os caminhos da produção não capitalista. Lisboa: Edições Afrontamento, 2003. p. 21-66.

SCHWARTZ, Y. Le paradigme ergologique ou um métier de philosophe. Toulouse: Octanès Editions, 2000.

SEGURANÇA SOCIAL. IPSS/Iniciativas dos Particulares. 2008. Available at: http://195.245.197.202/left.asp?01.03. Accessed on: 19 may 2009.

SENAES. O que é Economia Solidária, 11 jul 2009. Ministério do Trabalho e Emprego, 2009.

SINGER, P. Economia socialista. In: SINGER, P.; MACHADO, J. (Ed.). Economia socialista: socialismo em discussão. São Paulo: Fundação

Perseu Abramo, 2000, p. 11-50.

SINGER, P. A recente ressurreição da economia solidária no Brasil. In: SANTOS, B. D. S. (Ed.). Produzir para viver: os caminhos da produção não capitalista. Lisboa: Edições Afrontamento, 2003. p. 71-107.

SINGER, P. Desenvolvimento capitalista e desenvolvimento solidário. Estudos Avançados, v. 18, n. 51, p. 7-22, may/aug 2004.

SINGER, P. A economia solidária vista a partir dos países do sul: Economia solidária no Brasil. In: Actas do Congresso internacional de economia solidária, Ponta Delgada. Centro de Estudos de Economia Solidária do Atlântico, 2005. p. 131-139.

SINGER, P. Brasil: El papel del Estado y de la sociedad. America Latina en movimiento, n. 430, p. 20-22, mar 2008.

SOUSA, G. M. F. d. As IPSS's, seu lugar em Portugal. Lisboa: Instituto Superior de Ciências do Trabalho e da Empresa, 2009.

TAYLOR, F. W. Shop Management. New York: Harper & Brothers, 1911.

TENDLER, S. Encontro com Milton Santos ou O Mundo Global Visto do Lado de Cá, 2007.

TITTONI, J. Subjetivação e trabalho: reflexões sobre a Economia Solidária. In: VIII Congresso Luso-Afro Brasileiro de Ciências Sociais, setembro 2004, Coimbra. Centro de Estudos Sociais, 2004.

UBERTI, L. Estudos pós-estruturalistas: entre aporias e contra-sensos? Educação e Realidade, v. 31, n. 2, p. 95-116, jul/dec 2006.

USSEN. The U.S. Solidarity Economy Network (SEN), 13 nov 2008.

VALENTIM, I. V. L. Economia Popular e Solidária no Brasil: uma questão de confiança interpessoal. In: XXIX Encontro da Associação Nacional de Pós-graduação e Pesquisa em Administração, Brasília. ANPAD, 2005.

VALENTIM, I. V. L. Are we fighting a single enemy? Looking for alternatives to capitalism with garbage workers. In: TITTENBRUN, J. (Ed.). Capitalism or Capitalisms? Szczecin: MyBook, 2009, p. 183-201.

VALENTIM, I. V. L. Economia Solidária nos Açores: um retrato de suas representações e construções midiáticas no Diário dos Açores. In: Anais do XI Congresso Ibero-Americano de Comunicação, 16-19 apr 2009, Funchal, 2009.

VALENTIM, I.V.L. Between Academic Pimping and Moral Harassment in

Higher Education: an Autoethnography in a Brazilian Public University. Journal of Academic Ethics, v. 16, p. 151–171, 2018. DOI: https://doi.org/10.1007/s10805-018-9300-y.

VALENTIM, I.V.L. Academic Pimping. In: Pensoneau-Conway S.L., Adams T.E., Bolen D.M. (Eds.). Doing Autoethnography. SensePublishers: Rotterdam, 2017. DOI: https://doi.org/10.1007/978-94-6351-158-2_18.

ZANETI, I. As sobras da modernidade. Porto Alegre, 2006.

INDEX

ABOUT THE AUTHOR

◀ Igor Vinicius Lima Valentim ▶

I was born in Rio de Janeiro, Brazil and had lived a nomadic life in places such as Porto Alegre, Balneário Camboriú, Itajaí, Criciúma, Ribeirão Preto, Itapiranga, Lisbon (Portugal) and Ponta Delgada – the capital of São Miguel island – in the Azores. I am currently associate professor at Federal University of Rio de Janeiro and at Fluminense Federal University Graduate Program in Education. I have written some books, chapters, and articles, and the topics that most catch my attention are: power, qualitative research, education, universities, subjectivities, interpersonal relationships, management, and trust. You can also find me on Medium platform.